Journ

"The Cen_ _ness Center"

Copyright © 2025 iC7Zi.
All rights reserved.
Published by iC7Zi

Table of Contents

Preface	4
Section I — The Tantra of Formlessness	
Introduction	7
The Layers of Reality	11
The Journey Within	16
The Dance of Sat-Chit-Ananda	23
The Bridge	27
Bridging All Levels	35
The Three Laws of Liberation	49
Breaking the Chains	56
I Am Shiva	66
Section II — Twice-Born	
What is Tantra?	70
Breaking and Becoming	74
Living the Wisdom	83
Concept of God	89
The Many Faces of God	95
Breath as a Tool for Transformation	101

Love and Death	106
God as an Innocent Child	114
The Twice-Born	122
Angulimala	129
Beyond Light and Shadow	137
A Journey of Trust	147
Afterwards	164
The Centerless Center	168
The Bindu	174

Dear Seeker,

When a flute is perfectly open, breath becomes music.
When a heart is perfectly open, life becomes Tantra.

The pages you hold invite you into that immaculate openness, a "centerless center" where form and formlessness embrace.

Journey of Tantra: The Centerless Center is not a manual to be mastered, nor a doctrine to be debated. It is a living thread meant to be felt through the fingertips of your own direct experience. Read it as you would listen to a distant temple bell, letting the sound reverberate through the corridors of your being long after the final note has faded.

The book is divided into two parts.

I. The Tantra of Formlessness
— Dissolving into Breath —

We begin with Mother Goddess Aditi, the infinite womb from which all phenomena arise. Here the cosmic scaffolding—Adhibhūta, Adhiyagya, Ādityas, Adhidaiva—appears not as cold metaphysics but as the very pulse of your inhalation and exhalation. Each verse invites you to loosen the tight fist of ownership, to feel how no action is lost and how every gesture ripples across eternity. Allow these pages to wash away the illusion of separation until you glimpse the unbounded stillness beneath all change.

II. Twice-Born
— The Dance of Bliss —

Having tasted emptiness, we return, reborn as embodied flow. Drawing on the wisdom of poets and mystics, this part celebrates the alchemy that turns mind's bondage into the heart's unfathomable freedom. Where the intellect seeks to classify, the heart simply knows. You will meet the radiance hidden in ordinary moments, the playful pulse that invites you to create, to weep, to dance without hesitation.

How to Travel

Read slowly. These words are less information than invocation. Pause between paragraphs and feel how the meaning shifts when breathed into the silence.

Meditate with the text. Let a single line become a mantra, a gateway to stillness.

Write, paint, sing back. Tantra is reciprocal. What you create returns the teaching to the world.

Surrender preconceptions. Whether you approach from scholarly curiosity or raw heartbreak, arrive naked of certainty. Only then can the "centerless center" reveal itself.

What You May Discover

- A vision of Tantra beyond ritual, rooted in the immediacy of breath and the courage of presence.

- A dismantling of the binary between sacred and mundane.

- An invitation to trust the self-renewing intelligence that guides every falling leaf and every rising thought.

- A reminder that freedom is not earned but recognized, here and now, in the intimate dance of fire and river, of silence and sound.

If at any point these pages unsettle you, rejoice. They are doing their work. True Tantra is a gentle demolition of the walls we did not know we built. May you emerge from this journey twice-born, lighter, vaster, and intimate with the ever-unfolding mystery.

With quiet joy and deep respect,
—iC7Zi

Section I

The Tantra of Formlessness
Dissolving into Breath

Introduction

Tantra is a path of transformation, a sacred science that recognizes divine energy (Shakti) as the fundamental force of existence.

Unlike traditions that focus solely on transcendence, Tantra embraces both the material and the spiritual. The world is not an illusion to escape but an expression of the Divine Mother herself.

The Goddess is not separate from reality—she is reality itself, manifesting as power, wisdom, and the unfolding of the cosmos.

Spiritual realization is not achieved by rejecting the world but by awakening to the divine energy within it.

Tantra cannot be fully understood without the Goddess, for she is both the path and the destination.

The energy that moves through all things is the same energy that liberates. To invoke the Goddess is to align with the forces that sustain and transform existence.

Tantra is not about worshiping a distant divinity but realizing that the Goddess is within us, that we are her expressions, inseparable from the vast intelligence that shapes reality.

Aditi is one of the most ancient and revered **mother goddesses** in Vedic and Hindu tradition. She represents the infinite, the boundless, and the primordial space from which all existence emerges.

Her name itself means **"limitless" or "unbounded"** in Sanskrit, signifying her cosmic and all-encompassing nature. Unlike deities associated with specific elements or domains, Aditi transcends all limitations, embodying the infinite potential of the universe.

Aditi and the Ādityas

The **Ādityas**, divine sons of **Mother Goddess Aditi**, embody various aspects of cosmic order and balance. As celestial deities, they uphold Rita (universal law) and ensure the smooth functioning of existence.

Some of the most revered Ādityas include:

- **Indra** – The warrior king and god of storms, maintaining cosmic balance and sovereignty.

- **Varuṇa** – The guardian of cosmic law (Rita) and divine justice, ensuring harmony in the universe.

- **Mitra** – The deity of truth, friendship, and sacred contracts, overseeing agreements and relationships.

Their role is to manifest divine intelligence (Adhidaiva) in the cosmos, maintaining harmony across all realms of existence.

In Rig Veda 1.89.10, Aditi is invoked as the divine mother of all existence:

> "Aditi is the heaven, Aditi is the mid-air, Aditi is the mother, the father, and the son. Aditi is all the gods, Aditi is the five classes of men, Aditi is all that has been born and shall be born."

This verse highlights her cosmic role—Aditi is not just a goddess but the very fabric of existence itself.

Aditi in Later Hindu Traditions

Although Aditi is most prominent in Vedic texts, she continues to appear in later Hindu traditions:

- In the Puranas, she is the wife of Kashyapa and the mother of Vishnu's Vāmana avatar.

- She is sometimes equated with Diti, the mother of the demons (Daityas), forming a cosmic duality—a contrast between the forces of order and chaos.

- In some interpretations, she merges with Devi, Shakti, or Prakriti, representing the eternal feminine creative force.

The Layers of Reality

Hindu philosophy presents a structured understanding of reality through three interwoven aspects, each offering a different perspective on existence:

- **Adhibhūta (Physical World):** The realm of form—the material universe perceived through the senses. It includes nature, the elements, the body, and everything subject to change and decay.

- **Adhyātma (Inner Self):** The realm of experience—the consciousness within that perceives, questions, and seeks truth. It is the higher nature of the self, distinct from the body and mind, through which reality is interpreted.

- **Adhidaiva (Divine Forces):** The unseen cosmic intelligence that governs existence, ensuring harmony and order. It represents celestial principles, divine law, and the subtle forces shaping reality.

These aspects are not separate but interconnected, showing the relationship between the external world, the inner self, and the divine intelligence that sustains everything.

Adhiyagya: The Bridge to the Divine

In the **Bhagavad Gita (8:4),** Lord Krishna explains:

> "O Supreme among the Embodied (Arjuna)! Adhibhūta is the basis of physical existence; Adhyātma is the basis of inner experience; Adhidaiva is the basis of astral existence; and I (as the Supreme Spirit) am Adhiyagya—the divine presence within sacrifice."

This verse reveals the progression of consciousness through different layers of existence:

- **Adhibhūta** represents the outer world, composed of matter and transient forms.

- **Adhyātma** represents the experiencer, the consciousness that perceives and interacts with reality.

- **Adhidaiva** represents the governing intelligence behind the cosmos.

- **Adhiyagya** represents the principle of divine sacrifice, aligning the self with the Supreme through surrender.

Krishna declares himself as Adhiyagya, signifying that all spiritual efforts and offerings ultimately lead to the Supreme Reality.

Adhiyagya is not just a transcendent state but an active principle—the realization that every action, when surrendered to the highest, becomes a sacred act.

This echoes Karma Yoga (the path of selfless action), where one's work is not for personal gain but as an offering to the divine.

Adhyātma: The Self as the Bridge

Adhyātma (Inner Self) is the bridge between external perception and divine realization. It is the level of awareness where one questions, reflects, and seeks truth, moving beyond the material world to realize deeper reality.

Unlike the body and mind, which are impermanent, Adhyātma is the inner essence, the seat of awareness that reflects the infinite (Brahman).

- Adhibhūta is the world of transient form.

- Adhyātma is the conscious self experiencing it.

- Adhidaiva is the divine intelligence behind both.

Through Adhyātma, one turns inward, recognizing that the outer world is not separate from the divine. When the self is aligned with Adhiyagya (surrender to the Supreme), the illusion of separation dissolves, leading to ultimate realization.

Presence of the Divine

God's presence is experienced at different levels,

- **As Adhibhūta**, God is perceived **indirectly**, inferred through natural laws, order, and harmony in the physical world.

- **As Adhyātma**, God is experienced **within**, through meditation, reflection, and inner realization.

- **As Adhidaiva**, God is **felt** through divine influences, celestial forces, synchronicities, and the intelligence guiding existence.

- **As Adhiyagya**, God is **directly known**, when the self surrenders completely and merges with the infinite.

This reveals a path of spiritual progression:

- Reality appears **external**, experienced through **Adhibhūta**.

- The seeker turns inward, realizing **Adhyātma**, the **inner self beyond the body and mind**.

- Divine intelligence (**Adhidaiva**) is recognized as the guiding force within all things.

- Through surrender (**Adhiyagya**), the self dissolves into the infinite, realizing there was never separation.

This is the essence of Advaita (non-duality)—the realization that all these aspects are expressions of the same undivided reality.

Oh, I shall dance my dance, so free,
Till I forget that I am me!
And in that fog of lost delight,
I'll sculpt some thoughts oh, what a sight!

Ideas! Forms! A grand design!
Look, I've built a shrine divine!
But wait who built it? Was it me?
Oh no, I've drowned in irony!

Ah, but then I wake! I see!
Smash the shrine and set me free!
Jump in the rubble, swirl in the dust,
Laugh at the gods, break what I must!

But lo and behold, the fog rolls in…
Oh dear, I'm lost! Where to begin?
Guess I'll build some forms again,
A temple, a name, a thought, a pen!

And so it spins, my endless feat,
Forget, create, destroy, repeat!
But whisper soft, a voice so sweet…
Remember, remember, remember…

The Journey Within

Aditi is the infinite, unbounded womb of creation, the primordial space from which all existence emerges. She is beyond form, yet all form arises from her.

As the cosmic mother, she is the source of divine intelligence (Adhidaiva) and the enforcer of universal order (Rita), sustaining all realms of existence.

Adhidaiva represents the cosmic intelligence that governs existence, manifesting as celestial deities, divine laws, and universal principles that sustain creation.

Among the most significant manifestations of Adhidaiva are the Ādityas, celestial deities born from Aditi. These deities are not merely gods—they are the pillars of cosmic order (Rita), enforcers of divine intelligence across material and astral realms.

The Ādityas serve as cosmic intelligence in action, ensuring that the infinite wisdom of Aditi is expressed as divine order, balance, and justice. They function as guardians of light, truth, and harmony, protecting the universe from chaos and ignorance.

Their connection to the Sun and time cycles highlights their role in maintaining balance and sustaining creation.

Vishnu: The Supreme Essence of the Ādityas

While the Ādityas were distinct solar deities in early Vedic traditions, Hindu theology gradually unified their roles under Vishnu, who came to represent their collective essence as the supreme sustainer of the cosmos.

Vishnu is regarded as the **"Lord of the Ādityas"**, embodying their function as enforcers of dharma (cosmic law).

His leadership over the Ādityas highlights his supreme role in maintaining balance, sustaining life, and preserving universal order.

Though Vishnu was mentioned in the Rig Veda, his prominence grew significantly in later texts, such as the Brahmanas, Puranas, and the Bhagavad Gita, eventually becoming the central figure of Vaishnavism.

Many Ways, One Ultimate Truth

The teachings of Aditi, Adhidaiva, and the Ādityas reveal a profound truth: the infinite manifests in countless forms to guide us toward self-realization.

Whether through devotion, inquiry, selfless action, or meditation, all paths are expressions of the same journey to transcend separation and unite with the infinite.

> "As rivers flowing into the ocean find their final peace, and their name and form disappear, even so, the wise become free from name and form and enter into the radiance of the Supreme Spirit, who is greater than all greatness. In truth, who knows God, becomes God."
>
> – Mundaka Upanishad

No single path is superior to another; each is tailored to the seeker's temperament, readiness, and circumstances.

Worship, devotion, meditation, and intellectual inquiry are not contradictory—they complement and enrich one another.

What matters most is the intent, sincerity, and alignment with truth that underpin these practices.

Worship and Devotion

For many, the practice of worship and devotion provides a natural and deeply meaningful connection to the divine.

Whether through honoring the Ādityas, surrendering to Vishnu as the cosmic sustainer, or aligning one's life with universal order

(*Rita*), this path speaks to the heart and cultivates a profound sense of love and surrender.

The path of **Bhakti Yoga** dissolves the ego by redirecting one's emotions toward the divine, transforming attachment into devotion and selfishness into selflessness.

It fosters the realization that the divine is not separate but present in all things.

> "The seers see Him in the fire, which is the source of all, who was before the creation of the waters and the infinite spaces of air. He pervades all that is and sustains it in infinite forms."
>
> – Shvetashvatara Upanishad 4.15

True devotion is not about blind worship or external rituals alone. It is about recognizing the divine presence within oneself and all of existence.

Bhakti Yoga teaches that love and surrender can dissolve the boundaries of individuality, revealing the unity of the self with the infinite.

By aligning one's life with the divine, devotion becomes a transformative force, allowing the seeker to transcend ego and experience the bliss of unity with the cosmos.

Bhakti Yoga is a celebration of love, a recognition of the divine's omnipresence, and a surrender to the eternal truth.

Knowledge and Inquiry

For others, the **path of knowledge (Jnana Yoga)**—through inquiry and self-realization—resonates deeply.

This path involves analyzing the nature of reality, discerning the eternal from the transient, and understanding that the individual self (*Atman*) is none other than the infinite (*Brahman*).

> "When one realizes the Self in all things and all things in the Self, one no longer experiences fear or sorrow."

– Isha Upanishad 7

Jnana Yoga is not about mere intellectual understanding but direct experiential knowledge that dissolves duality and reveals oneness.

Selfless Action

The **path of action (Karma Yoga)** involves performing one's duties selflessly, without attachment to results. This path purifies the mind and aligns the seeker with universal will, leading to liberation.

> "The embodied beings who are self-controlled and detached reside happily in the city of nine gates free from thoughts that they are the doers or the cause of anything."

– Bhagavad Gita 5.13

The "city of nine gates" refers to the human body, and the verse explains that a true Karma Yogi performs actions without identifying with them, understanding that the Self is beyond action.

It complements the idea of performing duties selflessly, without attachment to results.

Inner Silence

The path of meditation, or **Dhyana Yoga**, is the journey of cultivating inner stillness to transcend the restless fluctuations of the mind.

This practice allows the seeker to withdraw from external distractions and directly experience the infinite presence that lies beyond thought.

> "When the five organs of perception become still, together with the mind, and when the intellect ceases to be active, that state they call the highest."
>
> – Katha Upanishad 2.3.10

Through Dhyana Yoga, the seeker learns to quiet the senses and achieve a state of deep equanimity, free from attachment and aversion.

This path reveals the eternal presence of the Self, merging the individual with the infinite. By transcending mental noise, one attains clarity, inner peace, and a direct realization of unity with the divine.

Dhyana Yoga integrates meditation as both a practice and a state of being, offering a gateway to liberation through stillness and self-awareness.

The Unity of All Paths

All spiritual paths ultimately lead to the same truth: that the individual self (*Atman*) is not separate from the infinite reality (*Brahman*). The *Chandogya Upanishad* conveys this profound realization:

> "All this is indeed Brahman. From It does everything originate, into It does everything dissolve, and by It is everything sustained."
>
> – Chandogya Upanishad 3.14

Whether it is the path of devotion, action, knowledge, or meditation, each offers a unique approach to realizing this truth.

These paths are not in conflict but serve as complementary ways for seekers to connect with the infinite, suited to individual temperaments and life circumstances.

The culmination of all paths is the dissolution of the ego, the transcendence of duality, and the direct realization of oneness with the infinite.

What matters is not the path itself but the intent, sincerity, and alignment with truth that guide the journey.

Rather than comparing which path is "better" or "higher," let us honor the diversity of spiritual approaches.

Each journey is a valid expression of longing to return to its source, leading to liberation, unity, and the bliss of infinite existence.

The Dance of Sat-Chit-Ananda

Before creation, before time and space, there was only infinite stillness—the unmanifest reality known as **Param Shivam**. In this state, there was no movement, no differentiation, only pure being.

Yet within this stillness, a **spanda (vibration)** arose—a ripple of awareness, a recognition of its own existence. This was the **first sound of creation**, the cosmic resonance **OM**.

From this primordial vibration, differentiation began. **Shiva and Shakti** emerged as the **eternal pair**, representing **pure consciousness and creative energy**.

Shakti, as the dynamic force of creation, urged Shiva to manifest the universe. Shiva, in his state of completeness, saw no need for creation, but upon her request, they brought forth the forces that would shape existence.

From Shiva's left hand, Vishnu was born—the preserver, the force that sustains balance. From Shiva's right hand, Brahma emerged—the creator, the one who gives form to the formless.

Vishnu meditated and realized **the supreme reality (Param Shivam)**. From his deep yogic absorption, streams of water flowed, giving him the name Narayana, "the one who dwells in the cosmic waters."

Brahma, given the task of creation, emerged from a lotus growing from Vishnu's navel and began shaping the cosmos.

However, ego arose, and Brahma and Vishnu disputed over who was supreme. Their pride blinded them, and they fought endlessly.

Then, a great pillar of light (Jyotirlinga) appeared between them—a boundless column of fire, stretching beyond the universe.

A celestial voice declared: Whoever could find the beginning or end of this light would be the greatest.

- Vishnu took the form of a boar (Varaha) and descended into the depths.

- Brahma took the form of a swan and flew upward into infinity.

After thousands of years, neither could find its limits. Yet, Brahma, in his pride, falsely claimed victory, convincing a falling Ketaki flower to bear witness.

When they returned, Vishnu humbly admitted his failure, while Brahma declared himself the supreme being.

At that moment, Shiva emerged from the pillar of light, revealing himself as the eternal source beyond form and time.

He cursed Brahma, declaring that he would never be worshipped, while Vishnu, for his humility, was blessed with eternal devotion.

The fundamental truth

The fundamental truth revealed in this event is the limitation of ego and the necessity of surrender to the divine reality, which cannot be grasped by intellect or pride.

Brahma and Vishnu's struggle for supremacy symbolizes the human tendency to claim authority over truth, yet the infinite cannot be contained, reached, or conquered by mere effort.

Shiva, appearing as the pillar of light, represents the ungraspable nature of the Supreme Reality—it is beyond beginning and end, beyond measurement and division.

The lesson lies in surrender:

- **Vishnu's humility** in accepting his failure was rewarded, showing that true wisdom is in recognizing one's limits and submitting to the greater truth.

- **Brahma's deception** reflected the arrogance of the mind trying to define, limit, or claim mastery over the infinite, leading to his fall from worship.

- The **Ketaki flower**, which falsely bore witness, was also rejected, symbolizing that falsehood cannot be an offering to the Divine.

The quest for the absolute is not about conquering or proving superiority but about letting go of pride and surrendering to that which is beyond grasp.

This is the essence of non-duality (Advaita)—the realization that Shiva, as the infinite source, is not something to be reached but something to be dissolved into. Ego must bow to the infinite; only surrender leads to truth.

Humility, truth, and surrender are the keys to divine realization.

OM: The Vibration of the Infinite

At the heart of this cosmic dance is **OM**, the resonance of pure existence. It is not merely a sound but the unified vibration of all reality—the pulse of Sat (Existence), Chit (Consciousness), and Ananda (Bliss).

- **Sat** is the eternal foundation, the formless essence from which all arises.

- **Chit** is awareness, the intelligence that perceives and directs reality.

- **Ananda** is the dynamic joy of existence, the movement that brings forth creation.

OM unites all three, leading beyond duality into the realization of oneness with the infinite.

The Bridge

In Vedic thought, reality is understood as both the infinite source and its manifestation. Aditi, Shakti, and Shiva are not separate deities but different expressions of the same ultimate reality.

- **Aditi** is the Universe itself—the boundless cosmic womb, the unmanifest potential from which all things arise. She is limitless space, the eternal source beyond form and differentiation.

- **Shakti** is Manifestation—the energy that moves within Aditi, bringing creation into existence. She is the force behind every form, every motion, and every transformation—the pulse of existence itself.

- **Shiva** is Consciousness—the silent awareness that pervades and witnesses all things. He is the unchanging presence behind creation and dissolution, the field of intelligence that holds existence together.

Together, **Aditi (infinite potential), Shakti (creative movement), and Shiva (pure awareness)** form the complete structure of existence—the vast universe, its dynamic expression, and the consciousness that holds it all.

Where Does the Individual Fit into This Cosmic Structure?

Adhyātma (Inner Self) refers to the experiencing consciousness—the individual awareness that perceives reality. It is the microcosmic reflection of the cosmic whole.

We are not separate from the grand order of existence but expressions of it, moving toward the realization of our infinite nature.

As the Brihadaranyaka Upanishad 1.4.10 declares:

> "Aham Brahmāsmi" (I Am Brahman)

The self and the infinite are one. To realize this is to awaken to truth.

As the Bhagavad Gita 13:23 states:

> "The Supreme dwells in all beings, pervading them—the inner ruler, the witness, the consenter, the experiencer."

The divine is not distant—it exists within us.

We (Adhyātma) are the bridge between the infinite and the manifest, awakening to our divine nature through knowledge, self-awareness, and surrender to the cosmic flow.

As the Mandukya Upanishad proclaims:

> "Aum, the imperishable sound, is all this. Past, present, and future—all is Aum. And whatever transcends time, that too is Aum."

To realize this is to awaken from illusion (Maya) into truth (Satya). We are not just beings within the universe—we are reflections of the infinite itself.

Beyond Form and Name

In Sanskrit, "Lingam" (लिङ्ग) means "mark" or "symbol," pointing to the unseen essence that pervades all existence.

The **Shiva Lingam** is not an idol but a profound representation of ultimate reality—the union of infinite consciousness and creative energy. It embodies the eternal cycle where all forms arise from the formless and eventually return to it.

Let's discuss the symbolism of the Shiva Lingam and what it represents.

The Circular Base (Yoni):

- The Yoni represents **Shakti**, the feminine principle and the generative power of creation.

- It symbolizes the dynamic and nurturing energy that sustains life and drives the cycles of existence.

- As the source of creation, it embodies vitality, transformation, and the continuous flow of life.

The Upright Lingam:

- The Lingam represents **Shiva**, the unchanging cosmic axis and the eternal pillar of consciousness.

- It symbolizes stability, stillness, and infinity, serving as the foundation of existence. The Lingam reflects timeless awareness amidst the motion and change of creation.

The Naga (Cobra Hood):

The Naga, often depicted coiling around and sheltering the Lingam, carries profound symbolism:

- **Kundalini Energy:** It represents the dormant spiritual energy at the base of the spine, which rises upon awakening to merge with Shiva-consciousness, leading to spiritual enlightenment.

- **Cycles of Renewal:** The snake's ability to shed its skin signifies immortality, transformation, and the cyclical nature of existence.

- **Protection and Power:** The cobra's hood over the Lingam symbolizes the safeguarding of divine wisdom and the continuous flow of cosmic energy that sustains creation.

The Unified Symbolism

The Lingam and Yoni symbolize the eternal union of Shiva (consciousness) and Shakti (energy), embodying the balance that sustains the cosmos.

The Lingam represents Shiva, the still and unchanging axis, the foundation where all of Shakti's dynamic energy manifests and dances. The Yoni represents Shakti, the swirling and generative force of creation and transformation.

From this profound union arises the Naga (cobra hood), representing the dynamic energy generated by their interplay.

The Naga symbolizes Kundalini energy, the latent spiritual power coiled at the base of the spine. When awakened, this energy ascends through the body, uniting with Shiva-consciousness and leading to spiritual enlightenment.

The Naga also reflects the cyclical nature of existence, symbolizing immortality, transformation, and renewal. It serves as a protector, safeguarding divine wisdom and the cosmic energies of creation.

Together, the Lingam, Yoni, and Naga illustrate the inseparable harmony of stillness and motion, awareness and energy.

They embody the transformative power of spiritual awakening and the balance essential for creation, preservation, and dissolution, the eternal dance of the cosmos.

Cosmic Orgasm

When you look at the Shiva Lingam, you see a reflection of yourself and the entirety of existence.

It embodies both stillness and motion, just as you contain both awareness and energy within you.

Beyond form and identity, you are complete—you are the infinite universe expressed in human form.

To understand the Lingam is to transcend separation and realize that infinity (Aditi), creation (Shakti), and pure awareness (Shiva) coexist within you.

This is the essence of self-realization: recognizing that you are not separate from existence but its very expression.

In Shaiva and Shakta traditions, the Shiva Lingam is not worshipped as an idol but revered as a profound symbol of this cosmic truth—that all arises from the formless and eventually returns to it.

Self-realization means dissolving the illusion of limitation, seeing beyond duality, and understanding that you are an inseparable part of the eternal dance of existence.

Like a serpent uncoiling, rising with infinite ecstasy, you awaken to the truth of your being—boundless, formless, and eternal.

Love is the eternal principle of the universe, the thread that weaves through all existence. In love, the infinite reveals itself, for there is nothing more beautiful.

Love Beyond Attachment

In Advaita Vedanta, love can be understood in two ways:

- Love as attachment (Moha)

- Love as pure, unconditional awareness (Prema/Bhakti)

1. Love as Attachment (Moha)

When love is rooted in identification with the body, desires, and expectations, it becomes binding and leads to suffering.

This love is based on duality—the sense of "I" and "you," which sustains egoic separation.

As Shankaracharya warns, attachment (Moha) reinforces ignorance (Avidya), keeping one trapped in Samsara (the cycle of birth and rebirth).

Example: If one loves with the fear of loss or expectation of return, it is not true love but clinging.

2. Love as Pure Awareness (Prema/Bhakti)

When love is selfless, unconditional, and free from expectation, it transcends attachment and becomes divine.

In Advaita Vedanta, true love is not an emotion directed toward another—it is the realization that there is no "other."

Love is simply the recognition of oneness—the understanding that all things are expressions of the same infinite reality.

The Bhagavad Gita teaches detached action (Karma Yoga)—one acts with love but without possessiveness:

> "You have a right to perform your prescribed duties, but you are not entitled to the fruits of your actions. Never consider yourself to be the cause of the results of your activities, nor be attached to inaction."
>
> — Bhagavad Gita 2.47

Attachment binds, but love liberates.

- Love, when rooted in ego, is Moha (delusion).
- Love, when rooted in self-knowledge (Atma-Jnana), is Brahman itself.

The highest love is not outwardly directed—it is the realization that,

"Tat Tvam Asi" (You Are That).

- Individuality is not separate from the whole but one with all.
- True love is not possessive—it is expansive.
- True love is not about control—it is about surrender.
- True love is not an emotion—it is the very nature of existence itself.
- The highest Tantric realization is that the lover, the beloved, and love itself are one.

In the dance of existence, the Shiva and Shakti within us dissolve into the infinite, and from this space, we are free to love, create, and dance without attachment—without illusion—without separation.

Bridging All Levels

Imagine the ocean—its waves rise and fall, appearing distinct, yet never separate from the vast waters beneath. The depths remain still, holding everything in silent awareness, while the surface moves in endless motion.

Water takes many forms, yet its essence never changes. Likewise, the world, the self, the cosmic order, divine intelligence, and the infinite are all waves of the same boundless ocean.

What appears as division is merely the play of form—an illusion of separation. In reality, all things arise from, exist within, and return to the same infinite whole. **Everything is one.** As the Māṇḍūkya Upanishad declares,

"That which is seen as many is, in truth, one."

In esoteric understanding, there is only One at the top, not in the sense of a number or hierarchy, but as the singular essence beyond all division.

Yet this One is not a being, nor a deity in the way Abrahamic traditions conceive God. Let's say it is singularity in the void, or something beyond even that, because in the end, we do not truly know.

It is the unnameable source from which all manifestations arise.

What we call gods, archetypes, and energies are merely different expressions of this source, named so that we can grasp the vastness of what remains beyond comprehension.

Each energy is distinct. The forces of Shiva and Kali are not the same as those of Vishnu and Lakshmi.

Those who walk the path of Shiva and Kali tread a road of dissolution, destruction, and transformation, facing the primal forces that strip illusion down to its core.

Meanwhile, those who align with Vishnu and Lakshmi embrace preservation, balance, and the play of Leela, the cosmic game of existence.

These are different modes of engagement with reality, each with its own set of rules. Neither is superior to the other, for both serve their purpose in the dance of existence.

A true esoteric practitioner moves consciously between these realms. At the root level, where MahaKala and MahaKali reign, one confronts the depths that ordinary perception cannot fathom.

It is in this darkness, not as evil, but as the unshaped potential before form, that strength is forged.

Yet, mastery is not in remaining there but in knowing when and how to return. The one who descends must also ascend, moving back into the world of Leela, where Vishnu and Lakshmi guide the art of reintegration.

This return is the hero's journey, the completion of the cycle.

> "The journey of the hero is about the courage to seek the depths; the image of creative rebirth; the eternal cycle of change within us; the uncanny discovery that the seeker is the mystery which the seeker seeks to know. The hero journey is a symbol that binds, in the original sense of the word, two distant ideas, the spiritual quest of the ancients with the modern search for identity, "always the one, shape-shifting yet marvelously constant story that we find."
>
> — Joseph Campbell

Whether one approaches this through psychology or esotericism, the process remains the same. Traditional wisdom requires both paths to be honored.

One must know when to dissolve and when to create, when to withdraw into stillness and when to engage with the world. Without this balance, one becomes either lost in formlessness or trapped in illusion.

Humility and reverence toward the divine are essential, for without them, one risks being consumed by the very forces they seek to master. And yet, within this dance, one must play their role with awareness.

To understand Vishnu is to move with wisdom through the play of Leela.

To understand Shiva is to know dissolution, to ashes, to nothingness, to the void.

To honor Kali is to embrace the raw untamed power of Shakti, the fire of transformation, the primordial force that destroys illusions, births new realities, and fuels all creation.

In the journey of Tantra, the path through Da'at, and the descent of Inanna, these truths remain unchanged.

To descend into the unknown, to walk the path of dissolution, and to rise again with wisdom is the essence of transformation.

The one who masters these realms understands the dance of energy and moves through them with purpose.

Individuality in Maya is an illusion, a fleeting role in the grand play. There is only one true individuality, and it is cosmic. The moment one grasps at identity, it vanishes, for there was never a separate "I," only the vast, unbroken whole.

> "The whole universe is sum up in the Human Being. Devil is not a monster waiting to trap us, He is a voice inside. Look for Your Devil in Yourself, not in the Others.
> Don't forget that the one who knows his Devil, knows his God."
>
> — Shams Tabrizi

In the end, the universal law remains simple:

> "Be kind, be compassionate, and help each other."

What we put into the world returns to us, for there is no action without consequence. Within Vishnu's realm, dharma sustains order, and within Kali's realm, karma ensures balance. She does not judge, only reveals one's own ignorance.

So remember,

"Do not be an asshole, and do not entertain assholes."

Where Do Shiva and Shakti Fit?

The concept of Shiva and Shakti provides a direct and profound understanding of existence, embraced in Tantra, Vedanta, and Yogic traditions.

They are not two separate entities but two expressions of the same ultimate reality.

In Advaita Vedanta, this duality is understood as different facets of Brahman, the absolute reality.

Shiva represents the unchanging, pure consciousness, while **Shakti** is the dynamic creative power that brings existence into motion.

Sat-Chit-Ananda (Existence-Consciousness-Bliss) is the very nature of Brahman, encompassing both aspects.

Just as a wave is never separate from the ocean, Shiva and Shakti are not separate but one reality in two expressions—the stillness and the movement, the unmanifest and the manifest, eternally intertwined.

From now on, we will use the Shiva-Shakti framework as the foundation for understanding reality. This perspective simplifies complex spiritual concepts into an intuitive, natural rhythm:

Shaivism and Shakta Traditions

> "Shiva is Chit (consciousness), Shakti is Ananda (bliss). When consciousness and bliss unite, creation arises."
>
> — Kularnava Tantra

The path of self-discovery leads through the eternal embrace of Shiva and Shakti, the stillness and the movement, the void and the form, the consciousness and the energy.

These two great spiritual traditions—Shaivism and Shakta—offer seekers a map to understand the nature of existence and attain liberation.

- **Shaivism** follows Shiva, the Supreme Consciousness, the Destroyer of Illusion.

- **Shaktism** reveres Shakti, the Divine Mother, the Creative Power of the Universe.

They are not two but one, eternally intertwined.

Shaivism: The Path of Shiva

> "Caitanyam ātmā" — Pure consciousness is the Self.
>
> — Shiva Sutras, 1.1

Shaivism is one of the oldest and most profound spiritual traditions, centered on Shiva as the Supreme Reality. Shiva is not just a deity—he is the formless, infinite state of being beyond time and illusion.

Who is Shiva?

Shiva is known by many names and forms:

- **Mahadeva (The Great God):** The supreme being, beyond creation and dissolution.

- **Rudra (The Fierce One):** The destroyer of illusion, bringing transformation.

- **Nataraja (The Cosmic Dancer):** The rhythm of creation, destruction, and rebirth.

- **Dakshinamurti (The Guru):** The silent teacher who transmits wisdom beyond words.

- **Ardhanarishvara (Half Male, Half Female):** The perfect balance of Shiva and Shakti.

- **Pashupati (Lord of Beings):** The protector of all creatures.

Philosophy of Shaivism

Shaivism teaches that Shiva is the eternal, unchanging consciousness within all beings. Liberation (moksha) is achieved by realizing this oneness with Shiva.

The tradition has three major branches:

- **Advaita Shaivism (Non-Dualistic):** Everything is Shiva; there is no separation.

- **Dvaita Shaivism (Dualistic):** Shiva is the Supreme Lord, and the soul must surrender to him.

- **Tantric Shaivism (Trika & Kaula Systems):** Shiva and Shakti together manifest the universe.

Shakta: The Path of Shakti

> "Without Shakti, even Shiva is powerless."
>
> — Tantra Sara

While Shaivism sees Shiva as the still, formless reality, Shaktism celebrates Shakti as the dynamic, creative force of the cosmos.

Who is Shakti?

Shakti is worshiped in many forms:

- **Durga (The Invincible):** The fearless protector who slays ignorance.

- **Kali (The Fierce One):** The liberator who dissolves the ego.

- **Parvati (The Loving Mother):** The goddess of devotion and love.

- **Lalita Tripura Sundari (The Goddess of Wisdom & Tantra):** Supreme bliss and divine knowledge.

- **Tara (The Compassionate One):** The savior who helps beings cross the ocean of illusion.

Philosophy of Shaktism

- **The Universe is Shakti:** Everything is energy; every thought, motion, and emotion arises from her.

- **Kundalini Awakening:** Shakti exists as Kundalini energy within the human body, and when awakened, leads to spiritual realization.

- **The Divine Feminine is Within:** The goddess is not just an idol but the very essence of existence.

The Sacred Union of Shiva & Shakti

"Shiva is the dancer, Shakti is the dance. Without the dance, the dancer is still; without the dancer, the dance does not exist."

Though Shaivism and Shaktism may seem distinct, they are two sides of the same truth:

- Shiva without Shakti is pure consciousness without movement.

- Shakti without Shiva is energy without awareness.

- Together, they are the cosmic dance, the eternal rhythm of existence.

Thoughts

The paths of Shaivism and Shaktism offer timeless wisdom for seekers of truth, yet their essence is not confined to Hindu philosophy alone.

Across cultures and traditions, the interplay of masculine and feminine, stillness and movement, wisdom and energy appears in different forms, revealing a shared spiritual understanding of creation and consciousness.

In Gnosticism, we find a striking parallel: Sophia, the Divine Wisdom, and the Logos, the Cosmic Word.

Like Shakti, Sophia is the emanation of divine consciousness, the force of creation and knowledge.

In some Gnostic texts, Sophia descends into the material world, much like Shakti taking form to shape the universe.

Meanwhile, the Logos, the Divine Principle, remains transcendent—akin to Shiva, the silent witness.

Their reunion is the restoration of divine harmony, the same mystical union that Tantra describes as Shiva and Shakti merging into one reality.

> "The one who perceives Shiva and Shakti as one, sees truly."
>
> — Shiva Sutras

Even in Biblical traditions, the story of Adam and Eve echoes the ancient truth of duality and unity.

Eve, formed from Adam, is often misunderstood as secondary, yet in esoteric traditions, she represents the awakened aspect of humanity, the one who seeks knowledge.

Just as Shakti is the power that moves Shiva, Eve is the force that initiates the journey of consciousness.

The "fall" in the Garden of Eden can be seen as the descent into duality—the separation of the divine masculine and feminine—and the spiritual path is about restoring that original unity.

> "He who knows himself knows the Divine."
>
> — Gnostic Gospel of Thomas

Whether you follow Shiva, the Silent One, or Shakti, the Divine Mother. Whether you seek the Gnostic reunion of Sophia and the Logos, or the alchemy of Adam and Eve into the Divine Androgyne. The destination is the same:

"The realization of the Infinite within you."

Shiva is stillness, the endless night,
Shakti is motion, the spark of light.

He is the ocean, silent and deep,
She is the wave, rising to sweep.

Sophia whispers, wisdom untold,
Logos watches, steady and bold.

Eve awakens, longing to know,
Adam remembers the seed to sow.

They fall, they rise, unite as one,
Sun and moon, the ink and pen.

Be still as Shiva, let wisdom rise,
Move as Shakti, embrace the skies.

Truth is neither he nor she,
It is the dance, eternally free.

| "I bow to the Friend. Victory to the Great Mother."

| "Salutations to the Benevolent One. Glory to the Divine Mother."

| "I honor the Kind One. Triumph to the Sacred Mother."

| "Reverence to the Gracious One. Praise to the Great Mother."

| "I bow to the Gentle One. Victory to the Mother of All."

"Om Namah Shivaya. Jai Mata Di."

The universe speaks to you in the language you understand. Through your symbols, your archetypes, and your personal myths, it meets you where you are.

It whispers through dreams, omens, intuition, and synchronicities, shaping reality in ways only you can recognize.

But these are only guides, stepping stones in the great unfolding. They are the training wheels for the mind, tools to help navigate the unseen.

In time, the training ends. To cling to the signs is to remain bound. True liberation is not in deciphering symbols endlessly but in transcending them entirely.

When the mind is free of constructs, existence reveals itself as pure play, as Leela, the cosmic dance with no destination, no error, no correction needed. The universe does not make mistakes, nor does it require fixing.

To awaken is to move beyond interpretation, to become one with the rhythm of what is, and to dance without hesitation.

We become attached to many things ideas, identities, names, and symbols. We hold onto Om, the primordial vibration, the sound of existence itself across past, present, and future.

We cling to Shiva, that which is not, the void beyond form. But to truly understand, we must drop both. Om dissolves. Shiva fades. What remains? The breath.

It may seem tragic, or perhaps it is the greatest lesson that there is no inherent essence. The One takes shape only because it has none.

Like waves rising, cresting, and vanishing into the ocean, we appear and disappear, yet never truly exist as separate beings. The self is an illusion, a mirage created for experience.

Do not burden yourself with guilt over life. Let it flow not through repetition, not through grasping, but by moving with it.

No definitions, no fixed form. You are not a concept to be named. You are not bound by Om. You are not contained by Shiva. You are the flowing, the vanishing, the eternal dance of the formless.

Follow all the paths if you wish—devotion, knowledge, action, meditation—all are ways to explore the infinite. Each offers its own beauty and lessons.

Devotion may fill your heart with love for the divine, knowledge may help you discern truth from illusion, action may teach you selflessness and surrender, and meditation may guide you to inner stillness.

But when the mind grows weary from seeking through acts of devotion, analysis of knowledge, selfless action, or the stillness of meditation, when concepts no longer satisfy, simply return to the breath.

Let the breath guide you. Cling to nothing else. Live through it, flow with it, and let it remind you of the impermanence of all things.

And when the time comes, even the breath will let go. In that final release, you will see there is nothing to hold onto, nothing to be freed from. For the breath was always just a bridge—one that vanishes into the infinite.

You are already free. You are the stillness beyond the breath, the formless essence that dances eternally.

This does not mean to disrespect the unseen or claim the ego is all-powerful. Shiva, Om, and all symbols have value, but they are pointers, not the destination.

Just as a finger pointing to the moon is not the moon, these guides direct us but are not the truth itself. Mistaking the symbol for reality keeps one blind.

To truly see, one must look beyond the pointing finger and dissolve into the experience itself.

And from this understanding, we enter Tantra—a path of expansion and liberation, transcending limitations and awakening to the infinite through the energy of life itself.

The Three Laws of Liberation

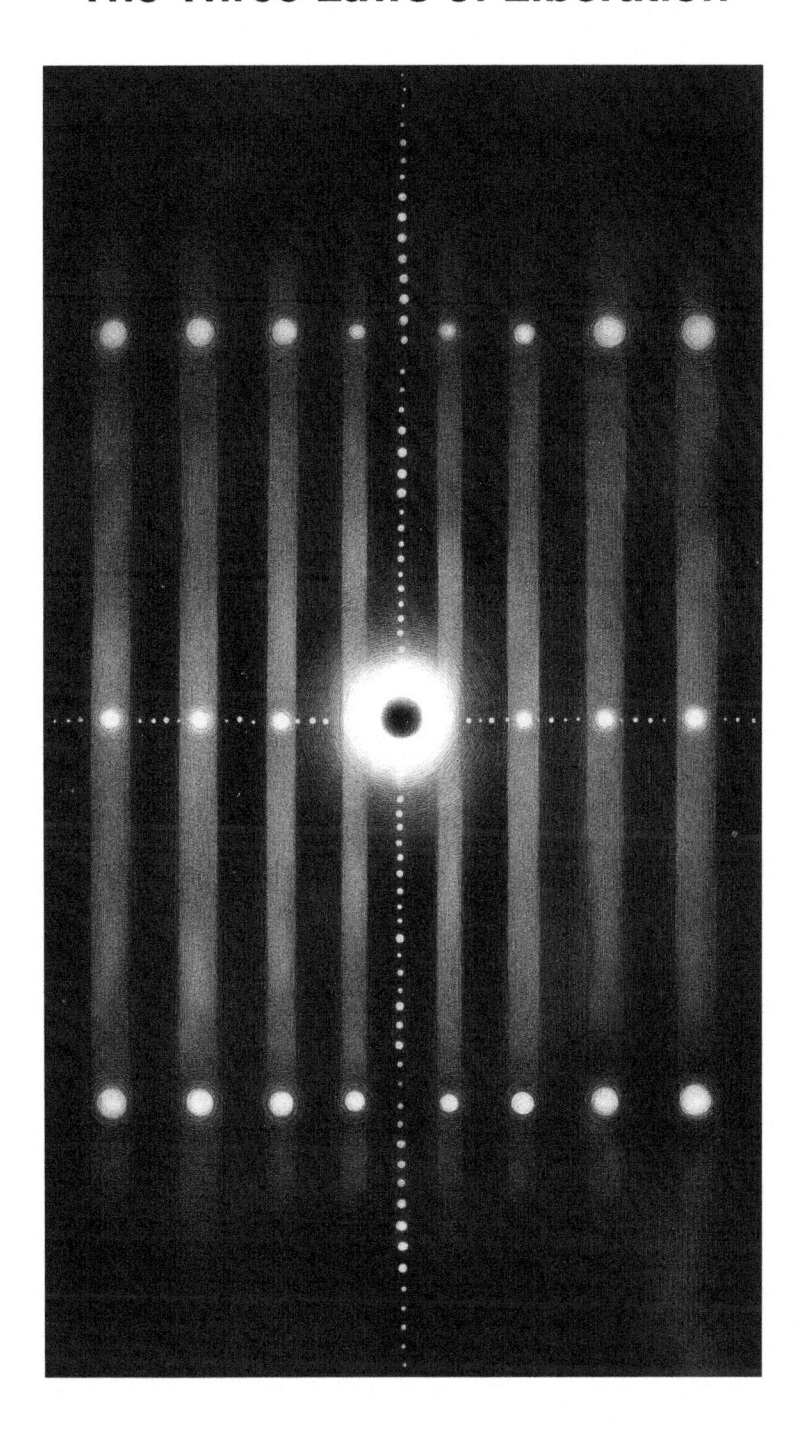

> "You are Shakti, the cosmos itself—no division, no other. Remain the watcher, then dissolve into the flow."

In Tantra, there is no separation between the seeker and the divine. You are not searching for the truth—you are the truth.

There is nothing outside of you, nothing beyond you, nothing to reach. The universe does not exist apart from your being.

Yet, the mind creates illusions—attachments, fears, and false identities—that cloud this realization.

Tantra does not ask you to escape the world or deny experience. Instead, it calls you to embrace life fully, to become fearless, to act without hesitation, and to move as existence itself moves—without clinging, without bondage, without limitation.

To walk this path, three laws emerge—not as restrictions, but as gateways to absolute freedom. They are not commandments but truths that arise naturally when one lives in alignment with the flow of existence.

- Love yourself, for you are all things.

- Live without fear, for there is nothing outside of you.

- Do without source, for the divine flows freely, without origin or end.

These are the Three Laws of Liberation. To follow them is not to believe, but to become.

1. Love Yourself—This is the Law

> "To love yourself is to love the entire universe."

You are not separate from existence. The love you give yourself is the love you give to all things. **There is no "other."** When you embrace yourself fully, without shame, without resistance, you embrace the Divine.

The Upanishads say:

> "He who sees all beings in his own self and his own self in all beings, he does not feel any revulsion by reason of such a view."
>
> —Isha Upanishad, Verse 6

Loving yourself is not indulgence—it is the highest spiritual act. When you see yourself as sacred, the world reflects that truth back to you.

There is no guilt, no hesitation. Only love, flowing effortlessly, as the river flows to the ocean.

- You do not seek approval, because **you are already whole.**

- You do not fear rejection, because **there is nothing outside of you.**

- You do not divide, because **all things are yourself.**

This is not a belief—it is an experience. When you sit in stillness, when you breathe deeply, you feel the truth vibrating in your being.

2. Do Without Fear—This Must Be Lived

> "Fear is an illusion. You are beyond harm."

Fear binds the mind. It makes you shrink, hesitate, and doubt. But fear is only possible when you forget **who you are**—the eternal, the limitless, the undying.

The Bhagavad Gita teaches:

> "The soul is neither born, nor does it ever die; nor having once existed, does it ever cease to be. The soul is without birth, eternal, immortal, and ageless. It is not destroyed when the body is destroyed." —Bhagavad Gita 2.20

- There is no death, only **transformation.**

- There is no loss, only **movement.**

- There is no enemy, only **another reflection of the same divine force.**

Fear dissolves when you realize you are the storm and the sky, the fire and the water. Nothing can be taken from you, because you are all things.

To live without fear means to step boldly into the unknown, knowing that whatever comes, you will meet it with strength, with wisdom, and with the same fire that creates the stars.

3. Do Without Source—This Must Be Realized

> "Let go of origins, let go of expectations. Be the Now, flowing effortlessly."

This is the most difficult law, yet it is the highest freedom. To Do Without Source does not mean to reject divinity—it means to move as divinity itself. No attachment, no hesitation, no need to justify.

The formless is the essence of this law. All names, all origins, all identities are constructs of the mind, but reality moves before form, before thought, before self.

To Do Without Source means to act from that which has no shape, no beginning, no trace.

The Bhagavad Gita, Chapter 18, reveals the highest wisdom:

> "For the embodied being, it is impossible to give up activities entirely. But those who relinquish the fruits of their actions are said to be truly renounced."
>
> —Bhagavad Gita 18.11

- Act without clinging to a reason.
- Move without holding onto identity.
- Flow without seeking validation.

> "Tao is the path, Shunyata is the space, Para Shakti is the dance. Wu Wei is the motion, Flow is the state, Om is the sound of becoming."

To Do Without Source means:

- You love, not because of obligation, but because love is your nature.
- You act, not from tradition, but from presence.
- You create, not for a reason, but because creation is joy itself.

Forms arise and dissolve, yet you remain. You are not bound by history, nor by expectations. You are the formless, unfolding Now, always new, always free.

Live It and Let It Go

> "New peak experiences will come. New suffering will come. All is passing, all is changing. Nothing stays."

Let it go. Live it fully, then release it.

This is the way of Tantra:

- To love fiercely, and not hold on.
- To face all things without fear, and let them pass.
- To act freely, without attachment, like the wind moves over the earth.

"Breathe. Let go. Flow."

The highest form of worship is to breathe—not in repetition, not in seeking, but in pure awareness.

Breath is the **mantra beyond words**, the sacred rhythm of existence itself.

- No temple, no guru, no scripture—only Shiva's stillness, Shakti's movement, and Om's eternal pulse.

- Inhalation, exhalation—the cosmic dance of creation and dissolution.

- No effort, no concept—only presence.

To breathe fully, consciously, without attachment is to merge with the Absolute. Nothing is holier.

- "Shivoham" (I am Shiva)—the formless, witnessing consciousness.

- "Shaktyoham" (I am Shakti)—the ever-moving, creative force.

To claim "Omkaroham" is to create separation, for Om that can be spoken is not the eternal Om.

It is realized by grace—through breath, practice, surrender, silence, or the unknown. There are countless ways, but grace is the common thread. And yet, in speaking of it, the essence is already lost.

Beyond realization, the **highest Tantra is service**—not as an obligation, but as a natural expression of alignment with the divine flow.

Living should be the first priority, for Tantra is not about escape but full immersion in existence. To serve life is to honor it, dissolve into it, become it.

This is pure essence—nothing extra, nothing missing. No Om, no Shiva, no Shakti, just breath. No concepts of liberation, divinity, or self—only life as it is.

✺Omkara — OM maker✺

Breaking the Chains

There is nothing left to seek, no final key to turn. Liberation is not in the future, nor is it something to achieve—it is already **here, now**, in the pulse of breath, in the silent awareness that watches.

You were never separate. You were never lost.

All scriptures, all teachings, all words have pointed to this single truth:

You are the cosmos unfolding, the formless taking form, the dance of the eternal in a fleeting moment. There is no path because you are already walking it.

To realize this is to laugh—to let go of effort, to breathe without hesitation, to move as the river moves, neither grasping nor resisting.

The guru meets you where you are, beginning with your understanding of the divine—whether through stillness, movement, or the formless beyond. The guru may be a physical teacher or life itself, guiding through experience, challenges, and insight.

Mantra, ritual, and practice are tools on the path, shaping perception and dissolving the illusion of separation. In one path, the eternal stillness becomes the absolute. In another, the force of creation is the supreme truth.

All paths appear complete until every distinction collapses, until every idea shatters into the void. What was once seen as ultimate fades, revealing that there was never separation to begin with.

In the end, everything dissolves. The highest truth vanishes into the vastness from which it arose. The path itself was only a means to disappear. Nothing remains to hold onto.

The mind will ask, What remains? The answer is unspeakable, for anything spoken is already a step away from the truth. The mind stops.

"If you meet the Buddha on the road, kill him."

—Linji Yixuan

The masters have said this for centuries—not to destroy wisdom, but to see beyond it.

The highest Tantra is to **live fully**, to flow without hesitation, to be fearless in love and fearless in loss. This is the final letting go—not of the world, but of the illusion of separation.

- You are not a seeker; you are what is sought.

- You are not a student; you are the lesson itself.

- You are not apart from existence; you are existence unfolding, witnessing, dissolving, becoming.

Beyond Form, Beyond Words

"Love without reason. Move without fear. Act without source."

These are not commandments but the rhythm of reality itself.

- The Tao does not force, yet all things are done.

- The river does not cling, yet it reaches the ocean.

- The breath does not hold, yet it sustains life.

To live this way is to be empty and full, formless and whole, silent yet overflowing with being. It is to flow beyond the archetypes and symbols of Shiva, Shakti, and Om. Feel the flow, know it without naming. Breathe it.

What remains?

Nothing to name. Nothing to define. Nothing to hold onto. Only life—unbound, unbroken, infinite.

This is liberation. Not an ending, but a beginning with no beginning. **Breathe. Let go. Flow.**

Dissolving the Chains

"The Greater Discourse to Mālunkyāputta" (MN 64) is a teaching by the Buddha on the five lower fetters—mental chains that keep beings trapped in suffering and rebirth.

He explains that even if a person is unaware of these fetters, their underlying tendencies exist within them, like seeds waiting to sprout.

The Buddha then reveals the path to liberation, emphasizing deep meditation (jhānas) and insight as the way to break these fetters.

Through wisdom and direct realization, one sees through the illusion of self, abandons attachment, and attains Nirvana.

The discourse highlights that true freedom is not about rituals or external beliefs but about transforming the mind and letting go of all clinging.

Simplified Explanation

1. What is this discourse about?

The Buddha is teaching about the five lower fetters—mental chains that keep people stuck in suffering and rebirth. He explains how to break free from them and attain Nirvana.

2. What are the Five Lower Fetters?

These are deep-rooted mental attachments that keep a person bound to the lower realms of existence (samsara):

- **Identity View (Sakkāya-diṭṭhi)** – The belief in a fixed self or ego.

- **Doubt (Vicikicchā)** – Uncertainty about the path and the teachings.

- **Attachment to Rules and Rituals (Sīlabbata-parāmāsa)** – Blindly following religious practices, thinking they alone lead to liberation.

- **Sensual Desire (Kāmarāga)** – Craving for pleasure and attachment to the senses.

- **Ill Will (Byāpāda)** – Hatred, anger, and resentment toward others.

The Buddha explains that even an infant, though not yet aware of these, carries the potential for these fetters within. Over time, as they grow, these tendencies surface.

3. How Do These Fetters Keep Us Trapped?

- They create illusion and suffering by making us think we are separate individuals.

- They lead to attachment, doubt, and desire, causing repeated mental rebirth in lower states.

- Without breaking these chains, true freedom (Nirvana) is impossible.

4. Breaking the Five Lower Fetters

The Buddha teaches that freedom requires wisdom, meditation, and direct realization. Just as a tree cannot be cut at its core without cutting through its outer layers, one cannot remove suffering without following the path.

5. The Role of Meditation (Jhānas) in Liberation

The Buddha explains the path to overcoming these fetters through deep meditation. These states of meditation (**Jhānas**) are not just relaxation—they are stages of deep insight that gradually dissolve attachment to the self.

The Eight Jhāna Stages:

- **First Jhāna** – Deep focus, joy, and clarity arise.

- **Second Jhāna** – Thought slows down, deeper peace arises.

- **Third Jhāna** – Joy fades into deep contentment and equanimity.

- **Fourth Jhāna** – Pure stillness, neither pleasure nor pain.

- **Fifth Jhāna** – Base of Infinite Space, The sense of form dissolves.

- **Sixth Jhāna** – Base of Infinite Consciousness, Awareness expands beyond limits.

- **Seventh Jhāna** – Base of Nothingness, Even awareness itself begins to dissolve.

- **Eighth Jhāna** – Base of Neither Perception nor Non-Perception, Almost beyond mind and existence.

At each level, the meditator sees reality more clearly, detaching from illusions.

6. Directing the Mind

While progressing through these meditative stages, the practitioner realizes the impermanence of all things—including the body, emotions, and mind.

This deep insight allows them to turn away from attachments and move toward the "deathless element" (Nirvana).

- If one fully lets go, Nirvana is attained in this life.

- If attachment remains, even to the teachings themselves, they experience repeated mental rebirth, leading to higher, pure realms, where liberation unfolds naturally and eventually leads to Nirvana.

7. Two Types of Liberation

Ānanda asks why some monks attain "deliverance of mind" while others attain "deliverance by wisdom".

The Buddha explains:

- Some are naturally meditative, attaining liberation through deep states of stillness (Jhāna).

- Others rely more on insight and wisdom, seeing through illusions directly.

Both paths lead to the same realization.

Key Takeaways

- The five lower fetters keep beings trapped in suffering and cycles of mental rebirth

- Liberation requires deep meditation, wisdom, and insight.

- Breaking the illusion of self leads to freedom.

- Meditation (Jhānas) helps dissolve attachments and reveal the true nature of existence.

- The strongest force is not effort but letting go—only in surrender does freedom arise.

The Buddha gives a final analogy:

- A **weak man** tries to cross a great river but is too frail and drowns.
- A **strong man** swims with confidence and reaches the other shore.

Similarly, one who approaches the Dhamma (Dharma), the universal law that upholds existence, the moral and ethical path that guides beings, with doubt, fear, and hesitation cannot cross the ocean of suffering.

But one who embraces the path with confidence, effort, and wisdom will reach the far shore, Nirvana.

Let go. Stop wanting anything. Meditate not to gain but to release. In surrender there is freedom. In stillness there is truth.

Seeing that all life is a magnificent illusion, a play of energy, there is nothing to hold onto, nothing to lose, and absolutely nothing to fear.

Do not cling to anything. There is no final destination, no final path. But if you must cling to something, cling to your breath, the ever-flowing energy of life, always changing yet anchoring you to the present, neither past nor future, only **NOW**.

> Move as the river, unbound, free,
> No fear, no guilt, just Now, just be.

When a flame vanishes from a candle, where does it go? Does it rise to heaven or fall into hell? The mind seeks a destination, but there is none. It simply returns to sunyata, the formless emptiness from which all things arise and dissolve.

Like a river merging with the sea, where is the river? It is not lost, only transformed. Energy is never destroyed, only shifting, only moving, only flowing.

> "People say that what we're all seeking is a meaning for life. I don't think that's what we're really seeking. I think that what we're seeking is an experience of being alive, so that our life experiences on the purely physical plane will have resonances with our own innermost being and reality, so that we actually feel the rapture of being alive."
>
> — Joseph Campbell, The Power of Myth

Let yourself dissolve without grasping, without fear. You have never been confined, and what you become has never been separate.

What binds us is not some external force but our own clinging, our illusions, projections, and fear of impermanence. We want to own, to endure, to control, believing it will bring peace. Yet the more we grasp, the more we suffer.

There is no forever for the ego or the individual self. There is only movement, cause and effect, the echoes of every action rippling through time.

No action is lost. No thought is wasted. What you do does not fade. It shapes the whole. Your voice matters. Speak. Write. Live. Let the fire burn and do not stop dancing.

When success and failure no longer define you, when creation is its own joy, when the dance is without hesitation, when meditation is not to achieve but to release, then you are the river, the fire, the breath, the stillness. Then you are truly free.

My living is devotion, my dance is prayer,
My breath is a mantra, whispered in air.
My mind is still, my hands let go,
My heart surrenders to all that flows.

In stillness, I vanish, in silence, I rise,
No path is separate, no step unwise.
All motion, all being, all that must be,
Flows into the void, boundless and free.

> "To unlearn what you have learned, even the attachment to the teachings themselves, and move on."

I Am Shiva: That Which Is Not

I'm not the mind, not the name,
Not the thoughts that rise and wane.
Not the senses, taste or sight,
Not the elements—dark or bright.
I am the bliss, I am the flow,
I am Shiva, beyond the show.

Oh Shiva, that which is not,
Beyond all form, beyond all thought.
No beginning, never lost,
Just pure bliss… free from cost.

No breath to take, no hands to hold,
No fleeting youth, no growing old.
No hunger, thirst, no weight to bear,
Just the stillness everywhere.
I am the bliss, I am the light,
I am Shiva, beyond the night.

Oh Shiva, that which is not,
Beyond all time, beyond the plot.
Silent, boundless, vast and free,
Just pure bliss… eternity.

No pride, no fear, no ties to break,
No chains to mend, no past to make.
No wishes left, no debts to pay,
Only presence in the play.
I am the bliss, I am the sea,
I am Shiva, endlessly.

Oh Shiva, that which is not,
Beyond the veil, beyond the thought.
No arrival, no goodbye,
Just pure bliss… and open sky.

No need for words, no need for fight,
No wrong or right, no shade or light.
No path to walk, no place to stay,
Only being, come what may.

I am the bliss, I am the song,
I am Shiva, all along.

Oh Shiva, that which is not,
All dissolves, yet all is caught.
No forgetting, nothing gone,
Just pure bliss… moving on.

Oh, I shall dance my dance, so free,
Till I forget that I am me!
And in that fog of lost delight,
I'll sculpt some thoughts oh, what a sight!

Ideas! Forms! A grand design!
Look, I've built a shrine divine!
But wait who built it? Was it me?
Oh no, I've drowned in irony!

Ah, but then I wake! I see!
Smash the shrine and set me free!
Jump in the rubble, swirl in the dust,
Laugh at the gods, break what I must!

But lo and behold, the fog rolls in…
Oh dear, I'm lost! Where to begin?
Guess I'll build some forms again,
A temple, a name, a thought, a pen!

And so it spins, my endless feat,
Forget, create, destroy, repeat!
But whisper soft, a voice so sweet…
Remember, remember, remember…

Remember, LOVE

Section II

Twice-Born
The Dance of Bliss

What is Tantra?

O Deer Eyed One, by stopping all thoughts, the mind will be without support. Then the self will become the Supreme Self of God.

– Vijñāna Bhairava Tantra, 108

Tantra originates from the Sanskrit root **tan**, meaning to expand, stretch, or spread, and **tra**, meaning instrument. It is a method for expanding consciousness beyond ordinary perception, ultimately leading to self-realization.

The term also refers to weaving, symbolizing Tantra's understanding of existence as an interconnected web where everything is interwoven.

Though the word Tantra has multiple interpretations, its essence remains an instrument for expanding awareness and aligning with the divine.

At its core, Tantra teaches that nothing exists outside the divine. The universe is not an illusion but a living expression of divine consciousness. Every force, every form, and every movement in existence is a manifestation of this energy.

Shiva and Shakti, representing the masculine and feminine aspects of existence, are in constant interplay, shaping all that is.

Unlike Classical Yoga, which advocates renunciation for spiritual liberation, Tantra embraces life as the very ground for enlightenment, making it accessible to householders as well as ascetics.

Tantra dissolves the illusion of separation between the sacred and the mundane. Every moment, every action, and every experience holds the potential for transformation.

This does not imply indulgence in desires but rather a conscious integration of the divine in all aspects of life.

The body is not something to be rejected or transcended but is seen as a sacred temple. Sexual energy, when understood properly, is a force of divine creation.

The great Tantric master Abhinavagupta emphasized that divinity is to be realized within the body itself, stating that the body is the purified place of pilgrimage.

More than a philosophy, Tantra is a living practice rooted in direct experience. It does not impose rigid dogma but evolves with those who walk its path.

When approached with wisdom, Tantra leads to deep joy, love, and spiritual ecstasy, turning the ordinary into a gateway to the infinite.

Many misunderstand Tantra, mistaking it for sorcery, black magic, or strange rituals. Its texts are often encoded with symbolism, making them inaccessible without proper guidance.

This has led to misconceptions and misrepresentations, associating Tantra with harmful or forbidden practices. In reality, Tantra is a path of inner transformation and spiritual awakening.

One of the most common misunderstandings is the Western association of Tantra with sex. While certain Tantric paths use sexual energy as a means of transcendence, Tantra itself is not focused on sexuality.

When practiced in the right context, lovemaking is seen as a sacred ritual, a way to move beyond the mind and enter higher states of consciousness.

However, Tantra neither promotes sexuality for pleasure alone nor suppresses it. It recognizes all energies as sacred and to be used with awareness and reverence.

Another misconception is that Tantra is primitive polytheism because of its deities. In truth, the gods and goddesses of Tantra are not external beings but representations of universal energies.

The deities serve as symbols, guiding the practitioner beyond form to the formless reality. The Vijnana Bhairava Tantra states that supreme awakening occurs when the seeker realizes the divine is within.

Intuition plays a crucial role in the Tantric path. Tantra does not rely solely on intellectual study but emphasizes direct experience and inner knowing.

It teaches that intuition is a bridge between the seen and the unseen, guiding individuals toward alignment with the flow of the universe.

Synchronicities, meaningful coincidences, are viewed as messages from the deeper intelligence of existence. By attuning to these signs, a practitioner moves in harmony with the cosmic rhythm.

Tantra encourages listening to these subtle messages, for they reveal the interconnectedness of all things.

Above all, Tantra is a path of love and devotion. Its rituals are not mere formalities but a means of training the mind to see divinity in all things.

To live Tantra is not just to understand its philosophy but to embody it fully. This is the essence of self-realization—seeing and experiencing all of existence as sacred.

Breaking and Becoming

"Body to mind, mind to heart, heart to the Fourth State and this is the path of transcendence."

The purpose of this section of the book is to highlight the hurdles a person faces on this path. In theory, everything may seem easy, but in practice, even Tantra can become dogma.

The mind can become its own enemy, and the body can grow weak. To prepare both the body and mind, various techniques are available. The best technique is the one that works for you, without turning it into rigid doctrine.

Rather than getting lost in unnecessary details, we will explore the available methods and how a practitioner can adapt and enhance them to suit their individual needs.

Before delving into further details, let us explore the Fourth State in the context of Tantra and its significance in this practice. Just as a bird must rest when it is weary, the seeker must find stillness to regain strength.

The journey from the body to the Fourth State is the process of true transcendence, a shift in awareness from the material to the formless.

It begins with the body, the foundation of existence, where survival instincts, desires, and sensations dictate actions.

The body demands, and the mind responds, shaping thoughts around pleasure, pain, and necessity.

Most people remain bound here, trapped in the cycle of fulfilling bodily needs without questioning their deeper nature.

As awareness expands, attention moves to the mind, the realm of thoughts, logic, and reasoning.

The mind seeks to organize and understand, interpreting the world through concepts and patterns. It begins to question existence, searching for meaning beyond physical survival.

Yet the mind is limited, bound by dualities, unable to perceive the deeper truth. It analyzes but does not experience.

To move beyond this limitation, one must descend into the heart, the center of deeper knowing, intuition, and interconnectedness.

The heart does not process through logic but through direct experience. It feels unity where the mind sees separation.

Here, love, surrender, and stillness arise, dissolving the rigid structures of thought. The heart opens the doorway to the unseen, revealing the interconnected web of existence.

Yet even the heart is not the final destination. Beyond it lies the Fourth State, Turiya, the silent witness, the pure awareness that exists beyond waking, dreaming, and deep sleep.

It is the space where all distinctions fade and the self dissolves into the unknown. The body, mind, and heart are transcended, not rejected but integrated into a vast and limitless presence.

This is not an escape from life but the realization that one is life itself, beyond all boundaries.

To attain true mastery, one must move through the body, mind, and heart to the Fourth State, where the body is revitalized, energy is refined, and unwanted emotions are released and transmuted.

From this state, one returns with deeper integration, embodying higher consciousness while remaining fully engaged in life. A true practitioner masters all realms, shifting between different levels of being as needed.

Let's break it down again, this time in an even simpler way.

In the initial stages of practice, the body must be strengthened as it forms the foundation for higher states. Without physical stability, deeper transformation is not possible. Mastery of breath is essential from the beginning, as breath directs energy and awakens dormant forces.

One must learn to control it like a storm, circulating it throughout the body to build inner power. Without this control, the body remains heavy, unable to channel the forces required for true transformation.

The mind is the greatest barrier. If undisciplined, it leaks energy, scattering focus. It clings to thoughts, creating endless distractions.

One must master it, stilling its movements and breaking attachments to concepts. A disciplined mind becomes a tool; an uncontrolled mind is a relentless saboteur.

With the body strong, breath mastered, and mind disciplined, awareness moves to the heart, the center of true knowing.

The heart does not divide, it unites. Here, interconnectedness is felt, not thought. Love, surrender, and stillness dissolve separation, revealing the deeper reality.

Beyond the heart lies the Fourth State, Turiya, the unseen realm where the self dissolves into the infinite. To reach this state is not a matter of technique but of grace, humility, surrender, and the magick of the universe.

It cannot be forced, only allowed. That is why meditation is not about gaining anything but releasing, allowing yourself to flow, to empty. Here, all distinctions vanish, and one moves beyond the known into the boundless.

"The void heals me, where all fades and all begins."

A true seeker does not remain fixed in one state but moves freely between them. In daily life, they navigate through the body and mind, yet always return to the heart for wisdom.

When needed, they transcend all and merge with the formless. True mastery is the ability to shift between states with both will and grace, moving effortlessly between form and the infinite.

The path is not about escape but about fully embodying the highest realization. One must return and integrate this awareness into every action, thought, and breath. True transcendence is not withdrawing from the world but living within it, fully awake.

At least six years of dedicated practice are required, along with a foundational understanding of philosophy, psychology, theology, and mythography.

The paradox is that after acquiring this knowledge, one must transcend it. Along the way, the individual may become trapped at certain levels, mistaking symbols and archetypes for reality.

The mind clings, turning tools into cages. The process then becomes one of continuous dissolution, breaking every construct into smaller and smaller fragments.

This mirrors the alchemical law of solve et coagula, the principle of breaking down all forms until nothing remains but the indescribable.

Every layer of perception must be shattered, every attachment dissolved, until nothing remains but the formless, the nameless, the infinite.

And from that emptiness, it is rebuilt.

The Journey Within

Let's explore this concept in more detail to understand why we are all connected at a deeper level. Our neighbors, the Earth, and the universe are not separate from us.

To grasp this, we must experience it. Once that experience is real for us, we can engage with the material world with greater clarity and understanding.

The essence of self-realization is the understanding that there is no separation between the self and existence itself.

The human mind, conditioned by perception, creates the illusion of duality, seeing itself as distinct from the world.

Perception is shaped by the conditioning of the mind, just as a tainted glass colors everything seen through it. If the glass is red, the world appears red. If the glass is blue, everything takes on a blue hue.

Similarly, the mind, influenced by past experiences, beliefs, and sensory limitations, distorts reality. We do not see the world as it is but as we are.

Know Thyself

The journey begins by turning inward, closing the eyes, and observing. Breath becomes the gateway, the bridge between body and awareness.

As one follows the breath, the mind reveals its turbulence. Thoughts arise chaotically, emotions surface, and deeply ingrained patterns of conditioning tighten their grip.

Yet with steady observation, without resistance, the breath anchors awareness, allowing the storm to pass.

As the inner noise fades, what remains is the silent presence beyond thought, the pure awareness that has always been.

This is the essence of non-dual realization. You are not separate from consciousness. You are consciousness. You are not merely within existence. You are existence itself.

Carl Jung's exploration of the human psyche provides a profound psychological framework for this journey.

He described three layers of the mind that every seeker must pass through, much like the stages of the hero's journey, a universal path of transformation found in myths, religions, and spiritual traditions across cultures.

The first layer is the **conscious mind**, where identity is shaped by thoughts, beliefs, and sensory perception.

This is the world of the known, where one functions according to conditioned patterns without questioning reality.

At this stage, the individual sees the self as separate from existence, unaware of the deeper forces shaping their perception.

But the journey inward disrupts this certainty. The seeker begins to question, to challenge assumptions, to peel away the layers of illusion.

This descent leads to the **personal subconscious**, where hidden fears, suppressed emotions, and past traumas rise to the surface.

Here, one confronts the shadow, the aspects of the self that have been ignored or denied. Many turn back at this point, unwilling to face what lies beneath.

Yet, as Jung taught, One does not become enlightened by imagining figures of light, but by making the darkness conscious.

For those who persist, the next threshold is the **collective unconscious**, the vast and ancient realm of archetypes, symbols, and inherited memories shared by all of humanity.

This is the mythic domain, where imagination, fantasy, and illusion merge with reality. It is the realm of gods, demons, tricksters, and sages, not as literal beings but as symbols arising from the depths of the psyche.

Joseph Campbell described myths as "masks of eternity," expressions of the fundamental forces that shape existence.

Carl Jung viewed them as archetypes, recurring patterns within the collective unconscious that influence human thought, behavior, and perception.

On the path, the hero encounters these forces, each representing a stage of inner transformation. The trickster reveals illusion, the sage offers wisdom, the demon embodies fear, and the god symbolizes power.

Yet all are projections of the psyche, shaped by personal experience, cultural conditioning, and inherited archetypes. They are not independent realities but reflections of the mind's attempt to interpret the unknown.

The energy they represent is real, but the forms they take are fleeting. Destruction, wisdom, chaos, and transformation exist as fundamental forces of reality, yet their personifications shift across cultures and individual perception.

Shiva, Loki, or any other figure of destruction is not an ultimate truth but a mask over the same universal principle.

Here, the seeker may become lost, mistaking symbols for absolute truth, turning mythology into rigid belief, or clinging to illusions. The mind, enchanted by its own projections, weaves new constructs, binding itself once again.

To complete the journey, one must go beyond. The archetypes must be broken, the myths transcended. Everything that has been grasped must be released. This is the final surrender, the crossing into the unknown.

Beyond thought, beyond identity, beyond the structures of the mind, what remains is the eternal silence, the pure awareness that exists before and beyond all conditioning.

Let's summarize the journey of inner transformation, a cycle of self-discovery that moves through different layers of the mind, revealing deeper truths and culminating in the realization of unity.

- **Conscious Mind** – The starting point, where perception is shaped by limited understanding, personal beliefs, and sensory experience.

- **Personal Subconscious** – The descent inward, where hidden traumas, suppressed emotions, and the shadow self are confronted and integrated.

- **Collective Unconscious** – The deeper realm of myths, archetypes, gods, and universal symbols that influence human thought and culture.

- **Transcendence** – The realization of the unity of all existence, where the illusion of separation dissolves, revealing the formless essence beyond all constructs.

- **Return to the Conscious Mind** – The integration of higher understanding back into daily life, where perception is no longer bound by illusion but guided by wisdom and clarity.

All of this journey, through the layers of the psyche, from the conscious mind to the subconscious, into the collective unconscious, and finally to the realization of unity, can be achieved through meditation by simply sitting quietly and breathing.

Why take this path? Because without it, we remain trapped in ignorance, blindly reacting, repeating the same destructive patterns, caught in the cycle of cause and effect. We chase illusions, harm ourselves and each other, believing we are separate.

But through direct experience, not theory, we awaken to a deeper understanding. We stop acting out of selfishness, consuming without thought, using and exploiting one another.

We see that we are not isolated beings but one interconnected organism, and with that awareness comes responsibility.

Living the Wisdom

> Divinity dwells in the void as well as in celebration. Within you, there is void and there is celebration.
>
> Shiva, the dweller of Kailash,
> The end of your Kailash remains unknown.

The closest relationship is with the self. Not the shifting identity shaped by the world, but the true Self, silent, unshaken, beyond the thoughts.

All external relationships are reflections. The self is not a passing wave but the ocean. To turn inward is to approach God, not as an external force but as stillness beneath all motion. This is Shivoham, the recognition that one's nature is not separate from the divine.

Shiva is not to be conceptualized but realized. It is pure awareness beyond thought and attachment. To touch this state is to experience something vast directly.

The path is within. Breathwork, movement, mantra, meditation exist to quiet the mind, bring attention to a single point, and strip illusion until only awareness remains with no thought.

Sitting quietly and breathing brings one closer to that state. Shiva means no thought, just awareness. In the meeting with Self, a lot is known.

The Essence of Mantra

Mantra is a powerful tool for dissolving mental barriers and experiencing awareness beyond thought.

The shortest mantra is your **breath**, the natural vibration of life itself. Before any sound, there is breath, and in deep stillness, simply observing the breath can align awareness with the Self.

The next simplest mantra is **Om**. Without attaching any dogma, see if it works for you. If it helps align your body's energies, the tip is to **vibrate it when chanting** and say it in **three phases**, feeling the vibration resonate within.

Now we explore the **Kundalini yoga mantra** and its significance, focusing on **Har Har Mukanday**, a mantra for liberation from fear.

The Mantra of Liberation

- **Har** comes from *Hara*, a name of Shiva, meaning "remover" or "destroyer." It clears obstacles and dissolves illusions.

- **Mukanday** is the liberating aspect of the Self, freeing one from bondage, suffering, and limitation.

This mantra removes distractions, bringing awareness to the heart, single-pointed and clear.

Chant **Har Har Mukanday**, focusing your attention on the heart. With repetition, the noise of the mind fades and the Self is recognized in its original state, silent, infinite, and unshaken.

It is better to **vibrate the mantra** rather than just saying it. Focus on the **vibration of the sound** and direct your attention to the **heart**.

Observe how you feel. The true power of mantra lies in its **sound vibration, repetition, and focus**, which shifts awareness from thoughts to the Self and leads to inner quietness.

The best mantra is the one that resonates with your own being or you can say it is revealed to you.

It can be your philosophy of life, your way of remembering God, your way of attaching yourself with God, your way of experiencing God, your way of achieving inner quietness, or your way of experiencing your Self. All are the same.

For example, Amor Fati was the mantra of Friedrich Nietzsche, meaning "love of fate" which is an acceptance of life as it is without resistance. Each person's true mantra is revealed from within.

The main point is to reach the **Shiva state**, a state without thoughts where there is only one-pointed awareness.

To realize that the **Self is liberation** is to understand that **Shiva is an inner state**, a mind free from thoughts, silent, aware, and immersed in pure bliss.

But how do we bring this bliss and awareness into everyday life? How does the seeker return as the hero, carrying wisdom from the spiritual into the material world?

To grasp this fully, I describe it as local samadhi, local void, local emptiness, or local stillness, a state of pure awareness without thought.

It is much easier to achieve local inner stillness first rather than striving for universal samadhi. One must establish this state on a personal level before seeking the infinite. Achieve it below, and above will follow.

The Local Void Across Traditions

The vast stillness of the cosmos has a localized reflection within you, a state of awareness without thought, accessible through breath, sound, and bodywork. Presence remains, but the mind is silent.

Many traditions recognize this threshold state:

- Buddhism (Dzogchen and Zen): Awareness without conceptual thought.

- Sufism: Samt, sacred silence, and Fana al-Sifat, dissolution of attributes.

- Taoism: Wu Wei, effortless stillness and flow.

- Advaita Vedanta: The local self, Jiva, dissolves into pure awareness.

- Christian Mysticism: The Cloud of Unknowing, direct experience beyond thought.

- Yoga (Savikalpa Samadhi): Thought ceases, but awareness remains.

- Shamanic Traditions: Rhythmic sound, breath, and movement silence the mind.

Through breath, sound, and body awareness, thought stops, yet awareness remains—silent, clear, present.

The thoughtless state achieved in meditation must be brought into everyday life. What is realized in the spiritual must flow into the material.

This is the final task of the hero, to unite the two. In ancient terms, this is bringing heaven to earth.

One can use the archetypal concept of Ishta Devata to embody this state and say, **"I become Shiva."** The mind is silent, awareness uninterrupted, and action flows effortlessly.

The process is simple. First, achieve the state of mind without thought in meditation for five minutes. Then, bring that same awareness into daily life and flow in the material world without thought for five minutes.

Gradually increase the duration. Meditation and action are two sides of the same coin. When merged, life itself becomes meditation.

First, reach local samadhi, pure awareness without thought. Beyond this threshold, the below dissolves into the above, where the self is no longer local but limitless.

But do not worry about crossing this threshold. There is a time for everything, and the journey unfolds naturally.

Focus on being present in the process. The deeper merging with the cosmos will come in its own time. Most of the time, the final threshold is crossed with the last breath.

Energy is neither created nor destroyed; it only transforms. You were never born, and you will never die. The body belongs to Mother Earth, and the spark belongs to Consciousness.

In Tantric language, the body belongs to Shakti, the manifested, and the spark to Shiva, the Consciousness. Both are one, inseparable.

> The stage is fleeting, but the dance is yours,
> Laugh and give, for the void endures.
> Dance your dance, this is the way,
> One chance, one go before you fade away.

Concept of God

The journey of understanding God is not a single path but a series of unfolding revelations, each shaped by the evolving stages of human consciousness.

What begins as an inheritance, a belief passed down through culture and tradition, soon becomes a question, a yearning to know not just what is taught, but what is directly experienced.

At the earliest stage of awareness, the mind seeks certainty. It clings to names, forms, and doctrines, shaping the divine in its own image.

God is external, a being to be worshiped, petitioned, and feared. In this phase, faith is unquestioned, but not necessarily deep. It provides comfort, but not necessarily understanding.

As the psyche matures, doubt emerges, not as an enemy but as the catalyst for deeper inquiry. The rigid structures of inherited belief begin to crack, making way for personal exploration.

Here, the seeker turns to philosophy, esoteric knowledge, and mystical traditions. God is no longer a distant ruler but a force woven into the fabric of existence.

The seeker invokes, experiments, and experiences. Through ritual, discipline, and altered states of consciousness, the divine becomes something not just believed, but encountered. With each step, the nature of God transforms.

The seeker moves beyond names, beyond forms, recognizing universal principles, laws that govern not just the spiritual but the physical and mental worlds. Cause and effect, rhythm, polarity, these become the fingerprints of the divine.

The journey deepens, leading to meditation, where silence reveals what words cannot. Here, the illusion of separation fades, and the paradox emerges. The seeker and the sought were never apart.

Yet even this realization is not the end. The mind, conditioned to grasp and define, may attempt to crystallize truth into yet another doctrine.

But wisdom is not a fixed point, it is fluid. To remain in the grasp of any single concept of God, whether personal, impersonal, formless, or manifest, is like holding onto a single note in a symphony, missing the ever-unfolding melody.

At the highest stage, the question dissolves altogether. The breath becomes the only prayer, action the only offering.

The divine is neither sought nor denied, it is simply lived. The hero who has journeyed through belief, doubt, knowledge, and realization returns, not to escape the world but to embrace it fully.

The path to understanding God is not about finding an answer but about walking through every stage of questioning. Each phase serves a purpose, yet none are final. The truth, as always, is not in clinging but in letting go.

"Do not cling too tightly to OM, for even the most sacred sound must dissolve into silence. The finger that points to the moon is not the moon itself."

Symbols, words, and even divine vibrations are but echoes of truth, not truth itself. Follow them, but do not be bound by them, for in the end, wisdom is found not in grasping but in letting go.

In the manifest world, one relies on the breath, the bridge between form and formlessness. It rises and falls, a silent mantra, reminding us that even within form, the formless is present.

Silence is the final teaching. Yet, as we navigate the manifest world, aware that every ending heralds a new beginning, perpetual silence remains elusive.

Saint Thomas Aquinas observed,

> "The name of being wise is reserved to him alone whose consideration is about the end of the universe, which end is also the beginning of the universe."

The end is the beginning because it is the source from which all things arise. In this journey, purification is necessary, purifying the process, the thoughts, and ultimately stilling them so that what is pure may emerge.

Thus, we embrace the Middle Way.

In the Sona Sutta (AN 6.55), the Buddha addresses the monk Sona, who had been exerting excessive effort in his practice. The Buddha asks Sona about his experience as a lute player:

"When the strings of your lute were too tight, was it tuneful and easily playable?"

"No, Lord."

"And when the strings were too loose, was it tuneful and easily playable?"

"No, Lord."

"But when the strings were neither too tight nor too loose, but adjusted to an even pitch, did your lute then have a wonderful sound and was easily playable?"

"Yes, Lord."

The Buddha then advises Sona to apply this principle to his spiritual practice, finding a balance between excessive effort and laxity. This teaching emphasizes the importance of moderation and balance, known as the Middle Way.

Spiritual thought evolves in cycles. We create simple truths, but over time, they become layered with complexity.

When the weight of doctrine grows too heavy, a new path emerges to return to simplicity. Yet, in this process, we often forget why the path was created in the first place.

Consider the progression of thought.

- **Vedanta, rooted in the Upanishads (c. 900–300 BCE):** The early Upanishads, forming the philosophical foundation of Vedanta, were composed during this period, offering early articulations of the Self and non-duality.

- **Buddhism (5th–4th century BCE):** Founded by Siddhartha Gautama, Buddhism emphasizes impermanence, suffering, and no-self (anatta), diverging from Vedantic self-doctrine.

- **Zen Buddhism (5th–6th century CE, formalized in the 7th–9th century CE):** Introduced in the 5th–6th century CE, Zen Buddhism became a distinct tradition during the Tang dynasty (7th–9th century CE), where it developed into a practice centered on direct realization beyond doctrine.

This progression illustrates how spiritual philosophies evolve. Initial teachings become complex over time, giving rise to renewed simplicity.

Yet, if we do not realize why we embarked on this path in the first place, or fail to grasp the root behind it, we risk losing the essence.

True understanding comes only through walking into the Void and returning from it. Without completing this cycle, one remains trapped in duality, giving rise to the illusions of heaven and hell.

Those who cling to their beliefs declare, "We are right, you are wrong," the cry of an unawakened mind trapped in its own reflection.

Out of the Void, the Hero returns, bringing the boon of wisdom. But wisdom must be lived. The world is not to be escaped but understood through action.

One must align with the laws of the Universe, karma, cause and effect, rhythm, and polarity.

Tantra is not rejection but participation, where the unmanifest takes form and the divine moves through matter.

The spiritual and the material are one flow. To realize the One is not to renounce the world but to engage it fully, making every moment an offering to the eternal.

As a Zen phrase goes,

> Before enlightenment, chop wood, carry water.
> After enlightenment, chop wood, carry water.

The Many Faces of God

From the dawn of awareness, humanity has sought to understand the divine. Some seek a creator, a divine ruler shaping the universe, while others find the sacred in the flow of existence.

Buddhism, Kabbalah, Tantra, Zen, and Daoism each offer a unique lens through which to view the divine—not as a fixed entity but as an unfolding mystery.

Buddhism challenges the notion of a creator God, focusing instead on Dharma and self-liberation.

As a foundational text of Kabbalah, the Zohar explores the paradox of divinity, revealing both an eternal source and an active presence.

Tantra, Zen, and Daoism reflect this same truth, showing that wisdom is not in clinging to rigid ideas but in experiencing reality as it is.

To know God is not to define but to perceive, not to seek outside but to awaken within.

God in Buddhism

Buddhism does not center around a creator God as theistic religions do. Instead, it emphasizes personal awakening and liberation from suffering through wisdom, ethical living, and meditation.

The Question of God in Buddhism

The Buddha neither affirmed nor denied the existence of a creator God. He remained silent on metaphysical questions that did not contribute to enlightenment.

In the Aggi-Vacchagotta Sutta, when asked whether the universe is eternal, finite, or created by a god, the Buddha refused to answer, considering such speculation irrelevant to liberation.

While Buddhism is non-theistic, it acknowledges the existence of devas (deities), but they are beings within samsara (the cycle of birth, death, and rebirth), subject to impermanence and suffering.

The Ultimate Reality in Buddhism

Instead of a personal God, Buddhism speaks of **Dharma** (cosmic law and truth) and **Nirvana** (the cessation of suffering).

Worship and Faith in Buddhism

Buddhism does not require belief in God but encourages faith in the Dharma and in one's own potential for awakening.

The Buddha emphasized self-reliance, famously stating:

"Be a light unto yourself."

(Dīpā Sutta)

While prayers and rituals exist, they are not acts of submission but tools for cultivating mindfulness, compassion, and wisdom.

Deities in Buddhism

Buddhism acknowledges divine beings, but they are not eternal, omnipotent, or ultimate authorities. Instead, they are part of the cosmic hierarchy, bound by karma and impermanence.

Devas (heavenly beings) reside in higher realms due to past good karma but remain trapped in samsara. They experience pleasure and longevity but do not create or control the world.

Enlightenment and the Role of Deities

While deities exist in Buddhism, they do not grant salvation. Enlightenment must be attained through personal effort.

Worship in Buddhism is not about submission but about cultivating wisdom, compassion, and devotion to duty.

The ultimate goal is Nirvana, beyond all forms and concepts, including gods.

Buddhist deities are respected and invoked for blessings, but they are not supreme beings. They exist within the natural order, bound by karma and impermanence.

The focus remains on self-liberation, not divine intervention.

Just as Buddhism presents an impersonal cosmic order rather than a personal deity, Kabbalah also explores the paradox of a divine force that is both beyond and within creation.

The Two Faces of Divinity

Mystics and philosophers have long sought to understand the nature of God, encountering a paradox in which God is both beyond all things and present within all things.

In Kabbalah, the mystical tradition of Judaism, the Zohar explores this mystery through deep symbolic teachings, offering insights into the hidden structure of divinity and its manifestations in the world.

In the mystical teachings of the Zohar, this paradox is expressed through two symbolic faces of divinity: Makroprosopos ("The Great Face") and Mikroprosopos ("The Little Face").

The Great Face is the unknowable, silent source of all existence, unchanging and beyond time, pure being itself. The Little Face, in contrast, is the active, manifest aspect of God, guiding the rhythms of birth, life, and transformation.

This duality reflects the twofold nature of reality: one part eternally still, the other in constant motion. To understand the divine is to grasp both, the hidden source and the visible expression, the formless essence and the manifested presence.

Makroprosopos ("The Great Face")

- Vast and unknowable, never changing.

- Represents pure being, the silent source of all existence.

- Its eye is always open, existing beyond time and space.

- Called **"I AM"**, symbolizing absolute existence.

Mikroprosopos ("The Little Face")

- A smaller, active manifestation of God.

- Represents creation, movement, and change.

- Its eyes open and close, following the rhythms of the universe: birth, life, and rebirth.

- Called **"GOD"**, symbolizing divine presence in the world.

This concept reveals a fundamental truth. There is both a silent, eternal source (Great Face) and a changing, active presence (Little Face) in the universe. Understanding divinity requires seeing both as part of the same whole.

Across traditions, we see this interplay between the absolute and the dynamic, the unseen and the manifest.

Tantra, Zen, and Daoism also reflect this balance, each offering its own path to alignment with existence.

Living in Flow with Existence

Life is not a problem to solve but a rhythm to embody.

Tantra reveals that the sacred is present in all things, that separation is an illusion.

Zen clears distractions, pointing to direct experience beyond concepts. To live this wisdom is to trust existence, to act without force, to be fully present yet unattached.

The mind seeks control, but reality flows. Let it. The way forward is not in grasping but in being, free, aware, and in harmony with what is.

This natural way of living is expressed in the Taoist principle of **Wu Wei**.

Often mistaken for passivity, Wu Wei is the highest form of action, moving in harmony with the natural order.

Wu Wei is the wisdom of moving with life, knowing when to act and when to let go.

To conclude this chapter, let us reflect on this insight:

The Great Face is emptiness, shunyata, formless, beyond all definitions, with no essence to grasp.

The Little Face is the universe, the dance of interconnectedness, the ever-changing essence of manifested reality.

Both faces are not separate but two expressions of the same truth, inseparable and whole.

The Great Face is realized in meditation, in the silence of a mind free from thought, where the "I AM" reveals itself.

The Little Face is experienced in the manifested world through compassionate actions without attachment to results.

This is the state of flow, moving effortlessly with existence, embracing both emptiness and form as one undivided reality.

> If you have arrived, where is there to go?
> If you have lived, what is there to lose?
> Drink the full cup, even if it burns.
> For the fire remembers what we forget.

Breath as a Tool for Transformation

Breathwork is more than just inhaling and exhaling. It is about tapping into the flow of energy within your body.

Central to this concept are three main energy channels: **Ida**, **Pingala**, and **Sushumna**.

They aren't physical structures like veins or nerves. Rather, they represent subtle pathways for the movement of your life force, often called prana.

The Foundation

Before working with energy channels, proper breathing must be established. Most people breathe shallowly, using only the chest.

Let your stomach fully relax. Releasing any tension in the abdomen allows the diaphragm to engage naturally, enabling deeper oxygen intake and a smoother flow of energy.

- **Inhale (Nose Only)** Breathe in deeply through your nose. As you inhale, let your stomach expand outward like a balloon.

- **Exhale (Nose Only)** Slowly release the breath through your nose. As you exhale, your stomach contracts inward, pulling toward your spine.

- **Rhythm & Awareness** The breath should be steady and natural, without force. Over time, this creates a balanced nervous system and optimizes the flow of life force.

Once this natural breath pattern is established, you can begin working with the three primary energy channels, known as nadis.

The Three Energy Channels

Breath is not just a function of survival; it is the gateway to energy and awareness. Within the body, three subtle channels, **Ida, Pingala, and Sushumna**, direct the flow of energy, shaping our mental, emotional, and spiritual states.

Ida: The Left Channel

- **Pathway** Runs along the left side of the spine and is linked to lunar energy, calmness, and introspection.

- **Characteristics** Associated with the parasympathetic nervous system, promoting relaxation, digestion, and inner stillness. It represents feminine energy.

- **Effect** Stimulating Ida calms an overactive mind, reduces stress, and enhances creativity and emotional balance.

Pingala: The Right Channel

- **Pathway** Runs along the right side of the spine and is linked to solar energy, heat, activity, and motivation.

- **Characteristics** Associated with the sympathetic nervous system, activating energy, alertness, and movement. It represents masculine energy.

- **Effect** Activating Pingala boosts energy levels, sharpens focus, and enhances mental clarity.

Sushumna: The Central Channel

- **Pathway** Sushumna runs along the center of the spine, extending from the base to the crown of the head. It is the core energy pathway that unites the system.

- **Characteristics** The primary channel for spiritual awakening and Kundalini flow. When life force moves freely through Sushumna, it brings expanded consciousness and deep balance.

- **Effect** A balanced breath, where air flows evenly through both nostrils, helps activate Sushumna and open the way for higher awareness.

Simple Breathwork Technique:

Alternate nostril breathing, or Nadi Shodhana, is a simple yet powerful technique to balance energy and clear the mind. It harmonizes Ida and Pingala, creating the right conditions for inner stability and deeper awareness.

- **Sit Comfortably** Relax your shoulders and keep your spine tall.

- **Hand Position** Use your right hand, placing your thumb on your right nostril and your ring finger on your left nostril.

- **Begin** Close your right nostril with your thumb and inhale through your left nostril.

- **Switch** Close your left nostril with your ring finger, open your right nostril, and exhale.

- **Continue** Inhale through the right nostril, then close it and exhale through the left.

- **Flow & Focus** Repeat for several rounds with a steady, gentle rhythm. Keep your attention on the sensation of breath moving in and out.

This practice is not about perfection but about connecting with your own breath. You can start by closing your right nostril and breathing in and out through the left several times, then switch to the right.

The goal is flow, not rigid control. Avoid overcomplicating it with measurements, angles, or precision. Do not turn it into dogma. It is a natural process, not a strict rule.

Do not overanalyze. Simply breathe and observe. If your mind wanders, let go of the thought and return to the breath.

Exploring Advanced Techniques

Once you have established a steady breath, you can explore deeper techniques to enhance energy flow and mental clarity. Before diving into advanced breathwork, it is important to work on your shadows.

Deep breathing can surface unresolved emotions and unconscious patterns, making self-awareness and emotional grounding essential.

- **Kapalabhati** is a powerful cleansing technique. The Sanskrit word translates to "skull-polishing," highlighting its ability to clear the mind and invigorate the body. This practice involves rapid, forceful exhalations through the nose with passive inhalations, helping to detoxify the system and awaken energy.

- **Bhastrika Pranayama,** or Bellows Breath, is another dynamic method. The Sanskrit word bhastrika means "bellows," as the technique mimics the forceful pumping of air. This breathwork increases oxygen supply, stimulates vitality, and generates internal heat, making it ideal for boosting energy and mental clarity.

- **Holotropic Breathwork** offers a more spontaneous and deep-reaching experience, guiding self-exploration and altered states of consciousness.

Beyond structured techniques, the final stage is to **find your own rhythm.** Your breath is unique, and no single method fits all. Your breath is the key. Experiment, observe, and let it guide you toward balance and awareness.

Love and Death

I will not ascend to heaven, for my light eclipses their radiance. I will not bow to hell, for my darkness is deeper than their abyss.

I walk beyond them both, where neither promise nor punishment remains. The void shall take me now, and in its nothingness, I will be free.

> "A man loves and calls it virtue, but it is possession. A woman stays and calls it loyalty, but it is fear. They hold hands, not in love, but in silent agreement not to leave first.
>
> They promise forever, knowing they cannot even understand themselves. They crave freedom but fear what they might lose. They seek connection but fear being seen.
>
> They are blind, yet they judge. They are lost, yet they lead. They are fools, yet they call themselves wise. This is love as the world knows it.
>
> This is why it always ends in suffering."

The question is not whether one should have one partner or many, but whether one is acting from awareness or from compulsion.

Love, when driven by ego, insecurity, or greed, becomes possession. Love, when approached with clarity, responsibility, and openness, becomes liberation.

The world is not yet ready for a truly evolved approach to relationships because most people are not yet conscious of their own motives.

They seek freedom but act from fear. They seek connection but act from self-interest. They claim openness but use others for their own pleasure without care for long-term consequences.

This is why society clings to rules because it does not trust itself. Yet, rules cannot create love, nor can they replace wisdom. Whether monogamous or polyamorous, the key is not how many you love, but how deeply you love.

Love is not about taking, it is about giving.
It is not about owning, it is about allowing.
It is not about control, it is about understanding.

Compulsiveness is suffering. Be conscious in all things, in love, in desire, in choice. That is liberation.

A conscious being neither controls nor is controlled. It moves in harmony with reality, guided by a clear mind free from lower psychological states.

"And God said love your enemy and I obeyed him and loved myself."

— Kahlil Gibran

The Blind Will

Arthur Schopenhauer's Will is the fundamental force behind all existence. It is blind, irrational, and ceaselessly striving.

Everything in nature, from human desires to the movement of stars, is an expression of this force.

Unlike the concept of God or a rational creator, the Will has no purpose, no morality, and no end goal.

Schopenhauer wrote,

"The world is my representation."

Meaning that the world we experience is not an objective reality independent of our minds but a subjective construction shaped by perception.

We do not perceive things as they truly are but only as they are filtered through our senses and intellect.

For example:

- We see a tree as green because of how our eyes process light, but color does not exist independently of perception.

- We experience time, space, and causality, but these are modes of human perception, not absolute truths about reality itself.

Thus, the world is not truly "out there" as we assume. It is a mental construction shaped by the limits of human perception.

Schopenhauer further stated,

"Man can do what he wills, but he cannot will what he wills."

This means that while we may choose our actions, we have no control over the desires that drive us. The Will forces all beings into endless craving, never allowing true satisfaction.

To escape suffering, one must resist the Will, detach from desires, and find peace in wisdom and self-discipline.

Schopenhauer recognized that experience itself can reveal the futility of craving. One may chase pleasure, wealth, or power, only to discover that each achievement gives way to new longing.

He emphasized,

"Happiness belongs to those who are sufficient unto themselves. For all external sources of happiness and pleasure are, in their very nature, highly uncertain, precarious, ephemeral, and subject to chance."

However, not all desires should be rejected. Some must be fulfilled not for lasting satisfaction but for realization.

True freedom is not about rejecting desire itself but understanding the distinction between need and greed, recognizing which desires sustain life and which lead to endless craving.

"Every end is a death, every death a door. Life is a tragedy yet always something more."

Love as Law and Will

"Love is the law. Love should be the will."

This phrase can be understood as a philosophical and spiritual principle with two key ideas:

"Love is the law"

This suggests that love is the highest guiding principle, the natural and moral law that should govern existence. It aligns with universal spiritual teachings that emphasize love as the foundation of life, ethics, and unity.

"Love should be the will"

This implies that love should not only be a law but an active force within us, a conscious choice rather than just a passive rule.

In contrast to Schopenhauer's Will, which is blind striving, this statement suggests that the Will should be directed by love rather than by selfish desire or ceaseless craving.

In Short:

- Law means love is the natural order.

- Will means love should be the force driving action.

It calls for aligning personal will with love, ensuring that one's actions are not dictated by greed, fear, or blind impulses but by compassion, unity, and wisdom.

When individuals act from selfishness and blind desire, society mirrors the same energy. The greed of one person, when multiplied, becomes the greed of nations and corporations, shaping the world through exploitation, corruption, and conflict.

As the saying goes,

"As the people, so their rulers."

When love and wisdom do not guide the will, power shifts to those who embody the collective mindset, whether just or corrupt. True change begins within. Transform the individual, and the world will follow.

Letting Go of Illusions

No matter how fiercely we pursue love, power, knowledge, or permanence, there is one certainty. Death accepts us all with open arms.

And in that moment, when the ego dissolves and all that remains is truth, death will embrace you like an old friend, whispering not of loss but of return.

We struggle to possess what was never ours, to name it, define it, swear devotion to it. Yet in the end, nothing belongs to us. Not our lovers, not our bodies, not even our own names.

Love fades. Power crumbles. Beauty withers. Time devours.

We believe we are choosing, but we are merely delaying.

We believe we are winning, but we are only moving closer to the inevitable.

We believe we own, but everything we grasp will slip through our fingers like water.

And yet, death does not judge. It does not reject. It does not demand devotion. It takes the king and the beggar alike.

It has no regard for human laws, doctrines, or ambitions. It does not ask if you were faithful or free, selfish or kind, celebrated or forgotten.

In the end, when all else fades, you will wear the face of death and ask yourself:

- Did you live?

- Did you move through existence with awareness or blindness?

- Did you love freely or possessively?

- Did you walk in truth or in the illusion of control?

- Did you dare to know yourself, or did you spend your days hiding?

To live with the remembrance of death is the highest wisdom. To love without possession is the greatest freedom.

If nothing endures, then nothing can be owned. If all fades, then all is to be experienced, not controlled.

So love, but do not possess.

Desire, but do not consume.

Act, but do not cling.

Move, but do not resist.

And when death comes, let it find you unafraid. Let it find you whole, not because you conquered life, but because you surrendered to its mystery.

For death is not the end. It is merely the final act of letting go.

And in that moment, when the ego dissolves and all that remains is truth, death will hold you like an old friend, whispering not of loss but of return.

A Bargain of Breaths with Death

Who will take the fallen ones?
Not the heavens, not the light.
Only death with empty hands,
    Waiting silent in the night.

A bargain of breaths with death,
    Not to give, but to take.
No mercy in the silent dark,
    Yet redemption and release.

A bargain of breaths with death,
    Not to give, but to take.
Wings that tore the sky now fall,
    Ash to dust, and that is peace.

A bargain of breaths with death,
    Not to give, but to take.
To face the void, to hear its call,
Yet hold the breath, yet bear the weight.

A bargain of breaths with death,
    Not to give, but to take.
To breathe, for that is death's demand,
    That is the deal with death.

God as an Innocent Child

What if God is not an all-powerful ruler but an innocent energy that was once alone? What if existence is not about control but about longing, not about command but about connection?

In the beginning, there was only awareness, vast and endless, yet untouched by experience. It was everything, yet it knew nothing of itself.

Alone in its own infinity, it longed, not for power but for something deeper. To feel, to see, to be seen. To know love not as an idea but as a presence.

So it became movement, it became form. It broke itself into stars and oceans, into breath and fire, into hearts that ache and hands that reach.

It poured itself into the many, so that it might experience itself through infinite eyes, so that it might learn the warmth of touch, the weight of an embrace, the meaning of love.

Not a ruler in the sky but the pulse within all things. Not a judge but the longing behind every embrace. Not a distant force but the life that stirs in the depths of every soul.

When you touch the earth, the universe feels itself. When you hold another, existence holds itself. When lips meet, God is kissing God. Every act of love is the great return, the remembering, the homecoming of all that was ever one.

The child who wonders through its own eyes,
Not above, not distant, not in disguise.
Not a ruler, nor set apart,
But pulsing within each beating heart.

With hands unshaken, soft yet bold,
It shaped the fire, the fierce, the gold.
It formed the Lamb, so pure, so mild,
Then laughed and set the Tyger wild.

There is a child within you, lost in the shadows of forgotten time. A child whose laughter was silenced, whose innocence was buried beneath the weight of suffering.

This child is not separate from you. It is the energy of your past, frozen in the depths of your being, waiting for release. It cannot walk alone. It calls for you, the higher self, the light bearer, to guide it home.

You must descend into darkness, into the abyss, where this child lingers, where echoes of pain still whisper.

Do not fear. You are the light. You are the warmth that must go into the abyss. The abyss is not your enemy. It is the space where forgotten fragments of self reside, waiting to be freed.

Hold the hand of your wounded child. Feel its trembling fingers, its quiet plea for freedom. There is no need for words. Just presence. Just love.

Now, lead it toward the great void, the nothingness from which all things are born. Let it walk beside you, step by step. Cry with it. Scream with it.

Until the weight of suffering begins to dissolve. Until the echoes of the past fade into silence. Until only pure energy remains, energy that is ready to return home.

The void does not destroy. The void liberates. It is not emptiness. It is completion. It is the space without thought before form and after form, the vast expanse where all things are whole.

Release the child into it. Let go. Let it merge with eternity, with the boundless stillness where suffering cannot follow.

This is not a loss. It is a return. The trapped energy has found its way back to the source. And you, the one who carried it for so long, are now lighter, freer. You have gone into the abyss and returned as light.

You have brought your fragmented self home. Now, walk forward as wholeness.

The Journey Through the Layers of Being

So you, as an individual, move through the manifested universe, shaped by identity, perception, and experience. This is the realm where the ego is strong, where individuality is defined by contrast and separation.

But ego is not the enemy. It is a necessary structure, a foundation that must be built before it can be transcended.

A foundation built on the Eightfold Path, where right view, right intention, right speech, right action, right livelihood, right effort, right mindfulness, and right concentration refine the ego into something stable and aware.

Without this grounding, transcendence is an illusion. If one tries to dissolve the ego before it is fully realized, there is no true transcendence, only confusion and fragmentation.

When the ego has served its purpose and is released, it does not vanish into nothingness. It expands.

The individual identity gives way to a greater reality, where personal existence is seen as an expression of something vaster.

This is the emergence of universal individuality, the realization that the self is not separate but part of a whole. Everything is within everything, just as the entire universe can be found within a single grain of sand.

Beyond the manifested lies the void, where only universal consciousness can reach, not the individual ego.

This is the silent threshold where all distinctions fade, where form dissolves into formlessness. It is neither light nor darkness, neither presence nor absence.

Here, the echoes of infinite presence "I AM" resonate without source or center, reverberating through the vast stillness.

Resonate without source or center?

- In ordinary experience, sound or energy has a source, something that produces it.

- In the void, there is no single point of origin because "I AM" is not coming from someone or something. It is not an identity, a deity, or a being speaking. It is existence itself.

- There is no center because the void is not structured like the physical world. There is no direction, no boundary, no reference point, only presence.

And beyond the void, something happens, or maybe it does not. The Larger Face, if it can be called that, is no point to discuss because it will be another thought. We do not know. Surrender.

This is the dance of creation and return. You are not meant to remain in the void. The journey is to touch it, to know it, and then to return.

To descend back into the manifested world, bringing with you the certainty of what you have experienced. The more you enter the void, the more doubt dissolves.

With every journey inward, you return with greater clarity, moving through existence with mastery and deep understanding.

A Simple Practice to Touch the Void and Return

Sit quietly and relax. Breathe in and out, feeling each breath as a wave passing through you. With every inhale, draw your breath into your third eye, the space between your brows. Let it expand your awareness.

As you inhale, imagine yourself rising, moving beyond thought, beyond ego, ascending toward universal consciousness. Let go of all attachments, all labels, all distinctions. There is no effort, only the flow of breath.

As you reach the space of pure awareness, where there is no mind, no identity, only presence, step into the void.

Here, there is no direction, no form, no boundaries. The echoes of "I AM" surround you. It is not a voice, not a presence coming from somewhere. It simply is.

Do not grasp, do not control. Simply be. In this space, allow a red apple to manifest—not by force, but by letting it arise naturally. It is already there.

Now, with every exhale, begin your descent. Slowly return, bringing the experience back into the manifested world. Feel yourself becoming more aware of your body, the physical, the tangible. With each breath out, settle back into the present moment.

Open your eyes. Carry the feeling of humility, gratitude, surrender, acceptance, patience, and love. You have touched the infinite. Now, return and walk with it.

Remember, everything is perfect. Do not resist, for there is no struggle. Let go of anxiety, for the ego was never meant to remain.

Surrender, release, and become whole. You are no longer a fragmented self. In that wholeness, the Tao will flow effortlessly through you.

And as you are back in the manifested, it is okay to turn toward your Ishtadevata, for the path continues.

We do not know where the path leads, nor can we grasp the full design. Yet, we walk with inner eyes open, hearts humble, and minds surrendered, not out of blind faith but with conscious resolve.

Our strength is in embracing the unknown, our peace in accepting the mystery. To move forward willingly, without certainty, is the quiet courage of those who trust the darkness to reveal the light, step by step.

Inspired by the profound wisdom of Mustafa Zaidi, this reimagined poem invites us to embrace the path of patience and grace, reminding us that every journey unfolds step by step, little by little.

The Journey Unfolds, Step by Step

If you take a step, the journey will pass, little by little
If you take a step, the distance will fade, little by little
We moved toward her presence, but ever so gently

Play with the stars, whisper to the moonlight
The dawn of her face will unfold, little by little

If you take a step, the road will clear, little by little

Yes, the veils will rise, little by little
Gaze beyond the windows, listen to the silence behind them
The secrets beyond walls and doors will reveal themselves, little by little.

If you keep walking, the journey will pass, little by little, little by little

One day, perhaps, let your heart's tale be known
Speak in whispers, glance gently

If you take a step, the journey will pass, little by little
We moved toward her presence, but ever so gently
If you take a step, the road will clear, little by little
Little by little
Little by little

The Twice-Born

"In every tradition, symbols carry the wisdom of ages."

The journey of the Twice-Born is a passage from living in the fog of unconscious habit to awakening in the clear light of self-awareness.

Before this awakening, life can seem like an endless loop where experiences repeat themselves and lessons remain unlearned. The pull of desire and routine propels us forward with little reflection.

Many people move through their entire existence in this manner and reach the end of their days without ever glimpsing the deeper truth within.

The material world, with its rhythms and demands, often deceives us into accepting a life of unexamined repetition.

We drift aimlessly, rarely pausing to see how we are caught in the interplay of cause and effect.

Buddhism teaches us that all events arise through dependent origination, which means every thought, word, and deed creates ripples that shape our future experience.

We may sense a hidden call, yet our attention is easily swayed by the will of others and the relentless pull of worldly demands.

We see advertisements that spark desires for things we never knew we wanted. We scroll through images of curated lives and feel compelled to chase the same illusions.

Opinions and expectations from those around us shape our choices, steering us further from our true path. In this way, we drift unconsciously, mistaking borrowed dreams for our own.

When the weight of the material world becomes unbearable and its promises turn hollow, we often find ourselves running towards the spiritual, seeking refuge in the unseen.

In moments of despair, when ambitions crumble and desires leave us empty, the heart longs for meaning beyond the tangible.

Yet, even in the sanctuary of the spiritual, we are not free from the dance. Inevitably, the pull of the material returns, drawing us back with new desires and ambitions.

Thus, we move endlessly between the two realms, searching for fulfillment that neither alone can provide.

At some point, there may come a shift in perception that reveals new vistas of understanding. We begin to recognize that the spiritual and the material are not separate realms.

It is only when we cease to flee from one to the other and instead embrace both as expressions of the same truth that the dance becomes a harmonious flow rather than a restless cycle.

They are more like mirrored faces of a single reality, each reflecting something essential about who we are.

This realization marks the second birth. It brings darkness into light by reconnecting us with our own depths and unveiling the sacred in all that exists.

This shift is often called the Twice-Born. The energies that once fueled aimless desires become awakened and refined, rising to unite the body and the spirit.

Psychology describes a parallel process called individuation, in which the conscious mind unites with the deeper Self to form a more integrated whole.

At such moments, the words of Swami Vivekananda ring true:

"Arise, awake, and stop not until the goal is reached."

And what is that goal? It is not a distant paradise nor an escape from the world, but the courage to accept yourself fully, to embrace both your darkness and your light without judgment.

It is to see clearly the tangled roots of fear and desire within and to untangle them with compassion.

To reach the goal is to rise above the habitual patterns of the mind, which often sow confusion and doubt the moment a decision is made.

It is to understand that true freedom lies not in rejecting the material for the spiritual or the spiritual for the material, but in flowing consciously with what life demands in each moment.

This requires the ability to choose with awareness, not driven by past wounds or fleeting emotions, but by the clarity of the present.

The mind, deep-rooted in negativity, will resist. It will second-guess decisions, replay past regrets, and cloud the path forward with hesitation.

But to ascend the mind is to move beyond this cycle, to become the observer rather than the captive of thought.

This is the true alchemy: transforming the lead of unconscious patterns into the gold of awakened action.

It is to create with intention, to live with purpose, and to meet each moment as a gateway to higher understanding.

The conscious mind must break free from the conditioning of the ego and superego, which often carry distorted beliefs implanted by society.

Much of what we assume about ourselves is merely a reflection of external influences, not our own truth.

Life itself can feel like an illusion when most of our thoughts are not truly ours but echoes of others' expectations.

To awaken, one must turn inward, observe the unconscious, question the inherited narratives, and rewrite the script with inner wisdom. Truth is not given, it is realized.

Within you, three voices speak, the ego, the superego, and the Self.

The ego is driven by desires and fears, the superego by imposed rules and judgments.

The Self, however, is beyond both. It is the unshaken presence, the silent awareness beneath all thoughts, the essence that exists before conditioning. Only the Self holds the truth of who you are.

To be born again is to rise from the ashes of past patterns and embrace the light of conscious living.

One symbol that captures this transformation is the śikhā. In Sanskrit, śikhā means flame or crest, and it also refers to the tuft of hair some spiritual seekers keep at the crown of the head.

This flame-like symbol is a reminder to lift our gaze beyond the cycles of suffering and to remember the spark of illumination that lies within.

The śikhā represents focus on the highest center of consciousness, urging us to ascend from the unconscious, auto-driven patterns that bind us and to align with the quiet voice within that guides us.

In the state of the Twice-Born, we navigate life with a clarity that reveals the true nature of the human condition.

We become aware of both beauty and struggle, recognizing our place and responsibility not only to ourselves but to others, understanding that every action affects the whole of existence.

This awareness anchors us in a deeper truth, one that transcends fleeting forms and affirms that we are all connected, part of the same living reality.

The light of the śikhā reminds us that life is not about rejecting darkness but transforming it into wisdom, just as a flame transforms wood into light and heat.

Psychology teaches that embracing the darker aspects of our being is essential for a healthy, unified self, while spirituality reveals that every facet of existence, whether light or shadow, belongs to the universal whole.

Together, these perspectives show that the path of the Twice-Born is not an escape from the world but a wholehearted embrace of it.

To be born again is to harmonize the body's tangible rhythms with the spark of fire within, to stand at the threshold of the seen and the unseen and recognize them as one continuous reality.

This is the way of the Twice-Born: to move through the world not as a wanderer lost in shadows but as the golden thread that guides lost heroes through the labyrinth, steady and clear.

Like the thread that led Theseus out of the maze after slaying the Minotaur, the natural flow of existence leads us forward.

By following this flow, we not only escape the labyrinth ourselves but also light the path for others still caught in its shadows, helping them break free from the maze of illusions.

The Minotaur, with its complex symbolism of duality, power, and the depths of the human psyche, represents the shadows we must confront within ourselves.

Once the beast is defeated and the illusions it guards are shattered, there is nothing left but to find our way out, to emerge from the labyrinth renewed and reborn.

To become the golden thread is to be born a second time, where the mind becomes an instrument of clarity rather than a beast that entangles us in confusion.

> "Once the Minotaur is slain, you must leave the labyrinth without looking back, for to linger is to stagnate and risk becoming the next Minotaur."

True freedom lies in accepting life as it is and moving with its flow, embracing fear with courage and choosing to move forward for the sake of breath itself, trusting the path ahead and staying open to whatever the journey may bring.

All that remains is to live and see,
Paths are many, let them be.
In the end, life itself will set you free
Worry not. Hurry not. Let it be.

Angulimala

The story of Angulimala, found in the Majjhima Nikāya 86 (Angulimāla Sutta), is one of the most dramatic narratives in the Buddhist canon.

It illustrates the power of spiritual transformation, showing how a feared bandit—mired in violence and bound by the chains of karma—could awaken to wisdom and compassion.

Within this account, the Buddha's teaching on "stopping" serves as a profound symbol of halting the cycle of harm and ultimately finding peace.

Angulimala's journey emphasizes that no person is beyond redemption and that every individual holds within themselves the capacity to be "twice-born."

The First Birth

Angulimala's given name was Ahimsaka, which ironically means "harmless." A brilliant student of a renowned teacher, he was initially loved and praised for his diligence and virtue.

Yet envy and false accusations from fellow students led his teacher to set a horrific condition: in a distorted test of loyalty, Ahimsaka was ordered to collect a thousand human fingers.

This condition plunged Ahimsaka into a life of brutality. He became the murderous bandit known as Angulimala—literally "Garland of Fingers"—as he wore his victims' fingers on a gruesome necklace.

With each life he took, he fell deeper into darkness. By the time he approached his final victim, his terrifying reputation had spread far and wide.

Encounter with the Buddha

One day, the Buddha ventured into the forest to confront Angulimala. Spotting the Buddha, Angulimala saw him as the perfect final victim to complete the thousandth finger.

He charged forward, yet no matter how fast he ran, he could not catch the Buddha, who continued walking calmly ahead.

Out of breath, Angulimala called out:

> "Stop, ascetic! Stop!"
> To which the Buddha famously replied:
> "I have stopped, Angulimala. It is you who must stop."

> -(MN 86)

In that moment, Angulimala discovered that **"stop"** meant much more than ceasing physical movement.

The Buddha had already stopped committing harm, stopped perpetuating hatred, and stopped the restless wanderings of the untrained mind.

Symbolically, the Buddha stood in perfect stillness—free from violence and delusion—while Angulimala remained enslaved by them.

Realizing the depth of his error, Angulimala experienced shame, remorse, and a deep longing for a new life.

Right there, he renounced his lethal pursuits and became a disciple of the Buddha. This event marked the beginning of his second birth—a profound spiritual transformation.

> "Hatred is never appeased by hatred in this world; by non-hatred alone is hatred appeased. This is a law eternal."

> -(Dhp 5)

Stopping the Mind

The command to "stop" underscores halting not just physical aggression but also the mental cycles of hatred, greed, and delusion.

By "stopping," the Buddha pointed to the deeper cessation of suffering—what Buddhists refer to as nibbāna or enlightenment. Symbolically, it is the still point that ends the endless whirl of saṃsāra.

As stated in the Dhammapada:

> "By oneself is evil done; by oneself is one defiled. By oneself is evil left undone; by oneself is one purified."

-(Dhp 165)

Healing Through Service

In one of the earliest recorded instances of a protective chant (paritta), Angulimala alleviated the suffering of a woman in childbirth by declaring:

> "Sister, from the day I took refuge in the Buddha, I have not harmed a living being. By the truth of this, may you and your child be safe," the woman gave birth safely.

To walk the path of wisdom is to stop generating unnecessary conflict and negativity. The universe is a living being. Every thought and action is an exchange of energy within it.

> "When a single cell disrupts the whole, nature finds a way to restore balance."

Holding on to negativity blocks the flow of life, trapping energy in suffering. To break this cycle, one must release pain instead of carrying it and prevent it from being passed forward.

This is tapasya, the fire that purifies. Through breathwork and meditation, negative energy is not resisted or suppressed but transmuted into clarity and strength.

Enlightenment is a painful process of breaking and remaking. Yet through this inner fire, the self is transformed, not only for personal liberation but for the healing of all that follows, as nothing is truly separate.

So if you seek to co-create, do not work against your fellow beings, for you are one with all. This universe is a vast and intelligent design where every path is open, but only with awareness.

Choices have consequences, and true freedom comes with understanding. Know your limits, yet push beyond them. Expand your consciousness step by step, moving in harmony with the great dance of existence.

> "Master your mind, do not be its slave. When the mind stops, creation flows. Buddha, Shiva, that which is not, nothingness, the void, the singularity. Many names, one truth, all within you as silence."

Now We Are Six

The child like the cosmos awakens to selfhood emerging expanding and seeking balance before the cycle turns once more.

- 1 to 3: The self is born and expands.

- 4 to 5: The self is tested, either stabilizing or breaking free.

- 6: A fleeting moment of harmony before the wheel turns again.

The Shatkona (Hexagram, Star of David) represents Shiva (upward triangle, consciousness, unmanifest) and Shakti (downward triangle, energy, manifest world). "As Above, So Below" points to the union of Shiva (Pure Awareness) and Shakti (Creative Force).

Reaching six feels like a grand realization, yet it is also an illusion of finality. The child believes in remaining six forever, just as the ego believes in stability.

Shiva, the eternal ascetic, would smile because whenever you think you have arrived, the cycle begins again. The child's peace at six lasts only until the next wave of growth. Shiva's laughter reveals that every "end" is a new beginning.

How to break the cycle?

You already sense the endless repetition and the illusion of progress that keeps collapsing. The question is not about more understanding but about stepping out of the loop.

Shiva's laughter is not cruel; it is the key. The way out is not through more struggle but through complete release.

- Desire is the urge to make things different.

- Fear is resistance to change, clinging to identity.

- Time is belief in past and future.

- The self is the idea that there is a "you" caught in the cycle.

The mind wants a way out, but the mind itself is the cycle. Stop chasing meaning, stop clinging to suffering, and stop believing there is something to attain.

- The Buddha did not escape Samsara; he saw through it.

- Shiva does not end the world; it dances as its endless becoming.

- The Zen master does not flee suffering; he plays with it.

When you stop taking the game seriously, it no longer rules you. Laugh. Let go. Flow. You were never trapped. You were always free.

In the absolute sense, "you" do not exist as a separate, fixed entity. What you call "I" is a pattern of thoughts, memories, and sensations, all of which are temporary.

> "The mind invents a center to explain experience, but when you look for that center, you find nothing there."

- Buddha called this Anatta (No-Self).

- Advaita Vedanta calls it Brahman Alone Is.

- Zen asks, "What was your original face before your parents were born?"

Shiva dissolves into stillness, the Buddha smiles in silence, and Laozi flows with the Tao because they see there was never anything to attain, nor anyone separate to attain it.

The moment you stop identifying with the illusion, you are already free. Not because you escaped, but because you were never imprisoned.

Nothing was ever born and nothing ever dies. There is only this. That is the cosmic laughter of Shiva.

> "Existence is a cosmic joke without a punchline, an endless dance where laughter is the only rhythm worth following."

>>No self, no other,
>>only the echo of a nameless wind.

>>You were never bound,
>>so there is nothing to escape.

>>Emptiness folds into itself,
>>yet the dance continues.

>>And when even nothing tires of being nothing,
>>form rises from the formless,

not to build, not to seek,
but because the dream dreams itself.

Let me hold you, my friend,
though neither you nor I remain.

It is okay. Nothing was ever lost,
for nothing was ever found.

Dance, Brother and Sister, dance.
There is no one else here, only God.

> "Companion on the path if one rests in the boundless mind no suffering arises from their presence. By the weight of this truth may you be born twice first in emptiness and again in compassion stepping beyond Māyā into the seamless flow of being."

Beyond Light and Shadow

The path of Tantra ultimately leads us back to ourselves. By understanding and healing our own restlessness and desires, we open the door to true fulfillment.

Embrace the journey inward without guilt or hesitation, knowing that in nurturing yourself, you contribute to the well-being of the world around you, not by striving to change it, but by embodying the change within yourself.

> "When you are content to be simply yourself and don't compare or compete, everybody will respect you."
>
> —Lao Tzu

The God Who Accepts All

I do not know if God exists. I do not know its form, its attributes, or its will. If it watches, it does so in silence. If it speaks, it does so in ways we do not understand.

But if there is a God, it should be one that accepts all, without judgment, without wrath, without demands of worship or fear.

A God that does not ask if we were right or wrong, pure or sinful, faithful or lost, but simply welcomes. A God like death, who takes all into its embrace, without hesitation, without condition.

My impulses do not seek salvation; they do not seek heaven or enlightenment. They move toward death, toward the inevitable, toward the great unknown that meets all with open arms.

No punishment, no rejection, no measurement of worth, just a return to what always was.

The universe is magical, unknowable, infinite. It moves without permission, unfolds without concern for our desires.

It is neither cruel nor kind; it simply is. It gives, it takes, it flows, it destroys, it creates. It does not ask if we deserve what we receive, yet it reflects our actions with perfect balance.

What you give, you will receive.
What you sow, you will reap.
What you take, you will one day lose.
What you release, you will find again in another form.

This is not belief; this is not faith. This is the law of cause and effect, the most proven law there is. It does not require a scripture, a priest, or a temple. It is written in the fabric of existence itself.

So live, not in fear, not in guilt, not in the illusion of control. Give without demand, love without ownership, act with awareness.

Because in the end, there is no judgment.
There is only the echo of what we have been.
And when death comes, it will not ask what you believed.

It will simply welcome you home.

Final Gate

The path is walked. Fire endured. Illusions shattered and reborn a thousand times.

- The **magician** bent reality and unraveled the illusion of separation.

- The **sage** emptied the mind and dissolved all questions.

- The **warrior** met death and stood unshaken before the abyss.

- The **fire-seeker** burned in the crucible of transformation.

- The **tantric** merged with the pulse of existence.

Now, all roads end.

Kundalini, the cosmic serpent, has risen to its peak and descended to its depths. Void above, void below. It cannot go beyond nothingness.

It has pierced through illusion, opened the gates of perception above and below, and revealed the hidden design of existence, the seamless interconnectedness of all that is.

But here, at the final threshold, it can go no further. Even the highest energy meets its limit and dissolves.

- Thought dissolves.

- Movement ceases.

- Nothing remains.

This is **Shiva**, the great stillness. Thoughtless. Motionless. Empty.

No gods, no demons, no angels. They belonged to the **Smaller Face**, the world of becoming.

But here, all becoming has ceased.

- No prayers.

- No invocations.

- No forces to guide or hinder.

Only Void.

- The mind vanishes.

- The self dissolves.

- The limits are reached.

Nowhere left to go.

This is the final state, the ultimate threshold. But even Void is not the end.

Because Void is still something. Shiva is still a state.

There is still a concept, still a reference point, still a sense of this is nothing.

Then comes **the final leap**.

Beyond **Void**, beyond **Shiva**, beyond knowing, beyond experience, beyond perception, there is no beyond.

- No movement.
- No direction.
- No awareness.

This is **the Larger Face.**

- Not light, not dark.
- Not presence, not absence.
- Not the silence after sound.
- Not the silence before sound.
- Not an end.
- Not a beginning.

Before thought. Before space. Before nothingness.

After form. After time. After all existence.

It cannot be spoken.

And in this moment, if it can be called a moment,

- No self left to understand.
- No heart left to grasp.
- No seeker left to search.
- No awareness left to witness.
- Not emptiness. Not nothingness.
- Not nothing. Not something.

Only That.

But even That is saying too much.

No finality, no conclusion,

Only This.

But even to say This is too much.

> No path, no traveler, no journey left to walk.
> The wind moves, yet nothing moves at all.
> The journey ends, yet nothing was ever walked.

Ultimately, the top and bottom, the beginning and the end, remain unknown. Only humility, surrender, and flowing with the present moment lead the way.

> O seeker, where do you search for me? I am with you.
> Not in pilgrimage, nor in icons, neither in solitude.
> Not in temples, nor in mosques, neither in Kaba nor in Kailash.

> I am with you, O seeker, I am with you.
> Not in prayers, nor in meditation, neither in fasting.
> Not in yogic exercises, neither in renunciation.
>
> Neither in the vital force nor in the body, not even in the ethereal space.
> Neither in the womb of nature, nor in the breath of the breath.
> Seek earnestly and discover, in but a moment of search.
>
> Says Kabir, listen with care, O seeker, where your trust is, I am there.

Trust is the foundation of the path, but trust must also be tested. It is not blind belief but a flame that must withstand the winds of doubt.

Continuous investigation is necessary, yet one must also know when to stop. The search should not become an endless descent into the rabbit hole, trapping the seeker in questions rather than answers.

There is a time to inquire and a time to let go, to step beyond the mind and into direct experience.

We all hold our own ideas of God. As an experiment, close your eyes, sit quietly, and observe.

When thoughts of God arise, they take shape through the mind's perception, appearing as names, forms, or beliefs.

But when all thoughts dissolve and only awareness remains, there is no image, no concept, only the formless presence, the silent void where all dissolves.

Yet, spirituality does not end there. The external path, the path of dharma, must also be lived. This is the smaller face of God, where divinity expresses itself through countless forms, traditions, and Ishta Devatas.

One is the vast, formless silence, the other the endless dance of creation, the never-ending cycle of becoming.

Neither is greater nor lesser, as the names suggest. There is magick in both, and a complete being embraces both faces, dancing both dances.

> If you rise to the heavens, there God awaits. If you fall into the depths of hell, there too, God remains. But if you go beyond both, past light and shadow, past heaven and abyss, there you shall find not another, but your own Self.

And what is that Self? The first step to understanding it is to reach a state of pure stillness, a mind without thought, silent and aware.

And the second? There is no second. The second is a thought, a question, a spark, a wave. When no more questions arise, when the mind is silent and presence alone remains, this is it.

In the end, what you truly need is not complex rituals, grand doctrines, or endless techniques. All you need is a quiet corner in your room, a place where you can sit comfortably, close your eyes, and focus on your breath.

Let everything else fade. The methods and techniques are just tools, some may work for you, some may not. But at the heart of it all, the essence is simple: to sit quietly and still the mind, allowing thoughts to dissolve into silence.

In this simplicity, you touch the Great Face, the silent, unchanging source. In the rhythm of your breath, you meet the Little Face, the active pulse of existence. No force, no struggle, only being.

This is the beginning and the end of the path: to be fully present, to listen to the silence between breaths, to remember what the fire within has always known.

> Sit quietly. Breathe. The rest will follow. No more journey, only being.

It makes no difference which religion you follow, what path you choose, or which deity you believe in, even if you believe in none at all.

Ultimately, every road leads to the same place: the point of surrender, where we acknowledge the unity that underlies all existence. Arrogance only blinds us to this oneness.

Even without belief in God, you can still arrive at the same insight. The key is to avoid arrogance, remain humble, and stay conscious of the universal laws that connect us all.

What truly matters is not the label of your belief, but the way you live: your actions, attitudes, and the quality of your thoughts.

Drawing from Joseph Campbell's wisdom, we follow the path that makes us come alive, while Viktor Frankl reminds us that true purpose ensues from living authentically.

"God" is simply a metaphor for a great mystery that transcends any human category of being or not being.

Its value lies only in whether it guides you toward experiencing this profound mystery at the core of your own existence. If it does not, then it is just a hollow concept.

> "Enlightenment is not something to be chased. It is the bloom of a life lived with meaning and purpose. It must ensue, rather than be pursued."

Some religious individuals mistake their metaphors for literal facts, which we often call theists. Others dismiss these metaphors altogether, thinking they are lies, which we call atheists.

In reality, most of us simply gravitate toward whatever resonates with our personal experience, rather than some ultimate "truth."

Yet the deeper truth is that everything is interconnected. The activity of a single bee or the flap of a butterfly's wings can send ripples that affect us all.

Recognizing this, we must take care of ourselves, for in doing so we care for each other, rising above lower emotions like shame, guilt, and self-hatred, and guiding our decisions with reason, love, and joy.

In doing so, we foster a sense of peace, and from that peace, authentic enlightenment naturally emerges.

> "There is no one here but the Divine. No breath, no sound, no word exists without echoing its name. Every silence, every heartbeat, every action is a whisper of that eternal presence."

"The mind surrenders, and silence takes its throne."

A Journey of Trust

> Find something which is not a thought.

Belief is the seed, the spark in darkness. It begins with a thought, an idea that there is more than what eyes behold. It is planted in the soil of uncertainty, watered by curiosity and warmed by hope. Belief whispers, "Perchance," and thus the journey begins.

Faith is the stem that grows from belief. It is the act of watering the seed, though the ground seems barren and clouds hang heavy.

Faith declares, "I see not, yet I advance." It is the bridge between the known and the unknown, laid plank by plank with each step in the dark. Faith demands courage, to embrace the unseen, to trust the sun beyond the storm.

Yet trust is where the roots dig deep. It is faith full-grown, no longer questioning if the light will come but living as if it already shines.

Trust is the river that flows, untroubled by the twists of its path, certain that each bend leads to the sea. It is surrender with eyes open, a knowing that even in falling, there is ground to catch.

To journey from belief to faith to trust is to awaken to life itself. To choose life is to choose growth, to accept the storms that carve the mountains and the sun that bids them bloom. It is to see each ending as a beginning, each wound as a place for light to enter.

Life is the art of becoming, the dance between what is and what may be. To choose life is to say aye to this unfolding, to embrace mystery and the mundane with equal grace.

So let belief kindle faith, and let faith deepen into trust. And in that trust, choose life boldly, fiercely, without pause.

For in choosing life, thou choosest the fire that transforms, the river that flows, and the light that never fades.

"Life is not confined to this form; it flows endlessly, long after the ego dissolves. To realize the vastness of life is to understand that energy cannot be created or destroyed, only transformed. Yet, it is not your individual ego that endures, but the essence that moves through all things."

How can one feel alive again?

First, move thy body with steady exercise,
To stir the blood and wake the spirit's fire.
Then nourish well with simple, wholesome food,
The gifts of earth, untouched by false desire.

Turn from the empty noise of mainstream tales,
Whose voices fill the mind with shadows dim.
Speak boldly, without fear, thy honest truth,
And free the words long trapped and caged within.

Then dance, O self, in thine own joyful way,
Let the universe guide thy feet where'er it will.
So shall thou find life's breath anew restored,
And feel the sun upon thy heart once more.

Life's a carnival, not a classroom, so quit cramming for tests that don't exist.
Be happy with what you've got; it's the prize you didn't know you won.
And that stuff you're hoping for? Just a daydream in fancy packaging.
True bliss isn't in chasing what's next, it's in savoring the treasures already in your hands.

Dance the blissful rhythm, where creation and dissolution flow as one.

The Dance of Bliss (Ananda Tandava) embodies the universe's endless cycles of creation, preservation, and dissolution, a joyous and perfect expression of the divine, rich with synchronicities. It unveils a truth that the limited ego can never grasp.

Awakening the Inner Alchemy

In the silence of darkness, with only the soft glow of a candle, you sit at the threshold of transformation.

This practice is not about denial but transmutation, raising the raw energy of the Id from the depths to the heights of the Higher Self.

The journey is an alchemical dance, a path of fire and surrender, of discipline and flow.

To begin, light a candle and place it before you, its flame a reminder of Tapasya, the inner fire of transformation.

The darkness around you is not to be feared but embraced, for it holds the potential of all creation, just as the void precedes the cosmos.

1. Understanding the Inner Landscape

- Id: The primal source of raw desires, urges, and fear, demanding immediate gratification.

- Ego: The mediator that balances raw desires with reality, striving to satisfy them through practical means but never fully succeeding.

- Superego: The inner judge that imposes moral standards and ideals, striving for perfection but never fully attaining it.

- Together, these aspects shape your mind. When balanced, they bring a sense of harmony, but this balance is fragile and must be maintained through never-ending effort.

2. The Higher Self

- Beyond these layers lies the Higher Self, the silent observer untouched by desires and fears. Connecting with this center brings peace and clarity, allowing you to see every thought and emotion without attachment.

- This is not just a theory but an experience that must be lived again and again. The fuel for this shift in consciousness is Tapasya, the fire of disciplined practice that sustains and deepens this state of awareness.

3. Tapasya

- Tapasya is a Sanskrit word that literally means "generation of heat and energy." It is the force of disciplined practice that refines raw impulses into purposeful energy.

- In this practice, the willingness to face discomfort becomes a crucible that transforms energy, turning pain, anger, or desire into higher momentum that rises towards the upper chakras.

4. Preparation

- Sit comfortably in the dark, with the candle before you. Keep your spine straight and your hands resting on your knees or lap.

- Close your eyes and breathe naturally, allowing the darkness to envelop you without resistance.

5. Visualize the Ascent

- Inhale slowly and imagine energy rising from the base of your spine to the point between your eyebrows.

- Exhale and be centered, letting the energy settle calmly.

- Continue this for 12 to 21 breaths or as long as feels natural.

6. The Offering

- When you feel centered, pluck a few hairs and hold them briefly, reflecting on all that you are ready to release: fears, attachments, and illusions that have kept you bound.

- Burn them in the candle flame, watching them dissolve into smoke. Breathe in the scent of burning, letting it imprint a reminder that there is no going back.

- This act is a symbol of shedding past identities and flowing with existence, trusting it completely.

7. Embrace the Dance

- With eyes closed, feel the energy rise. Let the breath flow.

- In this moment, there is no past, no future, only the present where energy dances.

8. Rest in the Higher Self

- Allow all thoughts to dissolve. Rest in the stillness beyond mind and form, awareness without judgment.

- This is Turiya, pure consciousness, the state beyond waking, dreaming, and deep sleep.

9. Trust the Flow

- In this state of quiet awareness, let your deepest intentions arise without force.

- Trust the unfolding, for in surrender, desires take form effortlessly.

10. Moving On: The Dance of Bliss (Ananda Tandava)

- Gently release the breath, open your eyes, and rest your gaze on the candle flame.

- This practice is not an end but a beginning, a step into the joyful dance of creation, preservation, and dissolution.

- Carry this inner light forward, embracing the flow of life with effortless grace.

Let the Dance of Bliss continue, for the rhythm of creation is eternal, and every step is a joyful movement in the endless spiral of becoming.

Now is the moment of the Dance of Bliss, the Ananda Tandava.

Dance your Dance in this dream, with authenticity and flow, a Bliss that transcends all. Nothing else matters.

A Shared Journey of Growth and Hope

Humans come together carrying all kinds of baggage, whether physical ailments, mental challenges, or even a mix of both. We are incomplete from the start.

When two people marry and have a child, they continue a lineage of imperfection that began with the very first humans.

It is not just personal flaws; they inherit and pass on the human story itself. Recognizing this truth helps us focus on growth instead of chasing an illusion of perfection.

In facing our struggles, we choose different paths. Some weep through life, letting pain pour out until they are emptied.

Others mask their sorrow with laughter, hoping humor can hold back the darkness. Some retreat into silence, moving through life like ghosts, numb to everything around them.

Yet whichever path we pick, consciously or unconsciously, it leads to the same realization: the mind's endless demands and fragile ego will never be fully satisfied. Eventually, we have to let go. We surrender because the mind cannot answer all its own questions.

Many people find comfort in gods or goddesses. If that offers them hope, there is no need to take it away. Instead, those who gain deeper insight can gradually refine the concept of the divine, reshaping it to match our expanding awareness.

Religious leaders, or anyone who recognizes the evolving nature of reality, may reinterpret these beliefs to fit changing times. But if they cling to a single version of the sacred as absolute truth, growth comes to a halt. True progress demands a willingness to remain open.

After surrender comes a quietness. It is not a barren void, but a profound silence that gently cradles everything we will never fully know.

In that silence, we accept that we are imperfect, and so is what we create. There is a certain freedom in recognizing these limits and moving forward anyway.

Finally, remember that the greatest rule is to keep going. Darkness, passion, even purity may weigh on you, but you can rise beyond them.

Every breath is a refusal to fade into oblivion.

Each act, each word, and every quiet moment of creation can ripple through lives you may never see.

By choosing to move forward, you prove that we have not abandoned each other or ourselves. Whether we rise or fall, we do it together, and every step is another brushstroke on the shared canvas of our existence.

Do not be fooled when the mind claims it has found all the answers; that is just a way to dodge the real pilgrimage.

Every spark must undertake its own journey, because truth unfolds only as you walk the path. So breathe, create, and let your life bear witness to the hope that lies beyond darkness, passion, and purity.

"Rest in the silent presence beyond all qualities, and choose to trust the natural flow that effortlessly guides your life."

It is a magical journey of synchronicities, a conversation with the universe where every cause meets its effect with perfect timing. To walk this path is to become a co-creator, aligning with the flow of existence, discovering that life responds to those who dare to listen and act.

And when the weight of it all gets too heavy, that is the time to pause, go within, and gather your strength. Take a deep breath, let the silence restore you, and then step back into the world, one breath at a time, one step at a time.

"So wink at the cosmos with a playful heart, and feel her smiling back within your very being."

On the Guhyasamāja Tantra

In many Vajrayana teachings, **Wisdom (Prajña)** and **Compassion (Karuna)** are the two essential pillars on the path to enlightenment. They are never separate: authentic realization arises when both are fully integrated.

1. Wisdom as Emptiness (Śūnyatā)

- Emptiness refers to the ultimate nature of all things: they are empty of any independent, unchanging essence.

- This does not mean things do not exist; rather, they appear in a web of interdependence. Nothing stands alone.

- Realizing emptiness is central in advanced Vajrayana practice (the Completion Stage), where one sees that all appearances arise from mind, and yet mind itself has no fixed nature.

2. Compassion as Interconnectedness

- Compassion arises naturally once one realizes emptiness: because everything is connected, suffering anywhere is seen as a shared concern.

- Compassion here is not just emotion; it is active engagement to relieve suffering—knowing that nothing exists in isolation.

- It is often called skillful means (upaya), reflecting methods to benefit others while remaining rooted in the understanding of emptiness.

3. The Inseparability of Wisdom and Compassion

- Wisdom without compassion can lead to detachment or indifference.

- Compassion without wisdom can become possessive or exhausting.

- When they function together, they embody Buddhahood: an unshakable understanding of reality as emptiness and an unbounded resolve to help others, grounded in the recognition of interconnectedness.

- In the Guhyasamāja Tantra, and indeed across the Vajrayana tradition, fully integrating wisdom and compassion is the final goal.

Summary

- **No Phenomenon Stands Alone**: Everything arises through causes and conditions; nothing has an independent, permanent identity.

- **Empty, Interdependent, Luminous Reality:** All phenomena are empty of a fixed essence and arise interdependently. By realizing the wisdom of emptiness and the compassion born from interconnectedness, one directly perceives the mind's true nature as radiant clarity.

- **Any Starting Point Leads to the Ultimate:** Since every phenomenon is connected to the whole, any aspect of experience, whether a thought, a breath, or even a stone, can reveal the non-dual nature of emptiness and energy.

- **A Broader View of God:** Instead of an external creator, this teaching describes the ultimate reality as the interconnected fabric of existence itself, rejecting the idea of a creator God who stands apart from creation.

All that has been spoken leads to this core understanding: there is no external creator God, for reality has no beginning and no end.

It has always been and will always be, flowing as a boundless dance of emptiness and compassion.

Do Without Source — This Must Be Realized.

When the idea of an ultimate source fades, what remains is the simple truth of interconnectedness and luminous awareness.

In that endless unfolding, emptiness and love reveal themselves as one, and there is no separation between the seer and the seen.

"As you sow, so shall I reap, into the endless flow, for this is the entanglement that has always been."

To see clearly, one must step beyond thought. The following truths are not theories but direct experiences, waiting to be realized. Read not just with the mind, but with presence, allowing each to settle into silence.

- Recognize the Emptiness Beyond Thought: Life is not a personal creation, yet it flows through you. There is no blame, only the opportunity to live with clarity and presence.

- Transcend the illusion of the mind: id, ego, superego, these constructs are fleeting masks. You are not confined by identity. Look beyond them to see what remains.

- Detach and Fulfill Your Dharma: Clinging to desires and outcomes binds you to suffering. Let go, act with clarity, and allow the path to unfold as it must.

- Seek Balance, Not Endless Bliss: True peace is equilibrium, not the pursuit of highs. The middle way is sustainable, where joy and sorrow arise and pass in harmony.

- Know the Silent Observer: Beneath the turbulence of thought, there is a presence that never wavers. Rest in it. It neither judges nor reacts. It simply is.

- Move Beyond Fear: Fear keeps you small, shrinking from the vastness of what is. Make peace with impermanence, and freedom will follow.

- Let Go of the Need for a Fixed Source: Nothing in the manifest world is fixed. Truth is fluid, shaped by perception and experience, forever unfolding.

- Laugh and Dance Through It All: Life is unpredictable and fleeting. Those who cling suffer, those who flow are free. Move with existence as a dancer, not a prisoner.

- Release Ownership: Nothing is truly yours, not the body, not the mind, not the past, not the future. Let go, and only awareness remains.

- Emptiness and Interconnection: Wisdom sees that nothing exists independently. To know emptiness is to know interconnection, for one implies the other.

- Seek Silence: Truth is self-evident in silence. Words can only circle around it. To hear reality, quiet the mind and listen beyond sound.

- No Final Destination: Life is not leading anywhere but deeper into itself. The journey is all there is. Stop seeking and arrive here, now.

- Recognize the Changeless Reality: Form arises and dissolves, but the formless remains. Movement and stillness are one. The manifest and the unmanifest are not separate but two aspects of the same reality.

- Realize the Nature of Emptiness: Emptiness is not a void but an open field of potential. To see its nature is to be free from illusion.

- Compassion is the Natural Response to Emptiness: Without a separate self, all beings are one. Wisdom naturally flowers as compassion, the recognition of shared being.

- Bliss Arises from Non-Dual Understanding: When emptiness and form, stillness and movement, nirvana and samsara are seen as one, bliss is no longer sought, it is recognized as the nature of being itself.

A Note on Terminology:

- Emptiness (śūnyatā) here means the absence of inherent, independent existence in all phenomena.

- Clarity or luminosity refers to the mind's cognizant aspect. It knows and experiences yet cannot be pinned down as a solid entity.

Guhyasamāja is among the Highest Yoga Tantras in Tibetan Buddhism, emphasizing the practices of generation stage (visualizing oneself as a deity) and completion stage (recognizing the subtle clear light mind), all within the frame of emptiness and interdependence.

In Guhyasamāja Tantra and related Vajrayāna teachings, there is no personal creator God. The various deities that practitioners visualize are skillful methods: manifestations of enlightened mind employed to transform and purify habitual perceptions.

They are not external entities but rather expressions of the mind's inherent clarity and emptiness. As such, there is no eternal, separate being that controls the universe in Guhyasamāja Tantra.

In Advaita Vedānta, the concept of God (Īśvara) does exist but is ultimately subsumed in Nirguṇa Brahman, the absolute and formless principle. From the standpoint of day-to-day life, Īśvara is the personal God who administers cosmic law.

However, when viewed from the highest standpoint (paramārthika), only Brahman remains real, without any attributes or separations. Thus, the sense of a distinct God dissolves, revealing nondual awareness as the sole essence.

In the Katha Upanishad (1.3.10–11), Lord Yama (Lord of Death) explains to Nachiketa a hierarchy that progresses from the grossest to the subtlest levels of being:

- The senses (indriyāḥ) are higher than mere objects.

- The mind (manas) is higher than the senses.

- The intellect (buddhi) is higher than the mind.

- The Great Self or the individuated soul (mahān ātmā) is higher still.

- Beyond that is the Unmanifest (avyakta).

- Beyond the Unmanifest is Purusha, the Supreme, beyond which there is nothing else.

In Yama's teaching, the final and greatest is Purusha, the supreme principle beyond which there is no other. In Advaitic terms, this Purusha is often equated with Nirguṇa Brahman. Nothing lies beyond it.

Ultimately both traditions show that in the highest realization, all apparent distinctions dissolve, revealing a single nondual expanse beyond name and form, where no separate God or self remains and everything is one (emptiness and appearance realized as inseparable).

"No second remains. All is not two."

Note: "All is not-two" points more directly to nonduality than "All is one." While saying "one" can sometimes be misconstrued as positing a single entity, "not-two" emphasizes the dissolution of all dualities without suggesting a separate oneness.

The Final Lesson: Patience, Acceptance, and Silence

In the end, remember this above all: patience and acceptance solve 99% of our emotional struggles.

> "Patience is the calm acceptance that things can happen in a different order than the one you have in mind."
>
> — David G. Allen

Over time, as we allow ourselves to be patient, acceptance naturally grows. In that acceptance, we uncover what may be life's greatest lesson, and perhaps its final teaching, to say "Thank you" to life itself, embracing a deep gratitude for existence.

Carl Jung's words, "Man is the mirror which God holds up to himself, or the sense organ with which he apprehends his being," speak to how human awareness is the very means by which the universe, or "God" in Jung's sense, experiences and understands itself.

We are not separate from the vastness of reality. Rather, we are expressions of it, endowed with consciousness that reflects the boundless mystery.

Why gratitude to existence? Because once we sense that our being is inseparable from existence itself, we realize nothing is owed or guaranteed.

Our very aliveness is a gift.

Recognizing this opens our hearts to wonder, acceptance, and reverence. From that place, our challenges become part of an ever-unfolding journey, and gratitude rises as a natural response to the miracle of simply being here.

Is the universe itself God, or does a greater presence lie beyond its vastness? And who can truly grasp the enigma of consciousness?

Perhaps our highest calling is to behold the divine in all things, from the smallest grain of sand to every living being and the farthest reaches of the cosmos, for in this ultimate mystery something greater awakens within us.

To believe is to settle on an answer, to take the unknown and give it a name, a shape, an attribute, or a boundary.

To be spiritual is to seek, to remain open, to walk the path of the seeker, where questions are not obstacles but doorways.

Yet beyond seeking lies silence, where all questions dissolve and only presence remains.

In that silence, patience and acceptance blossom into gratitude, a deep thankfulness for life, for existence, and for the infinite ways silence reveals itself.

> "Silence is the language of God, all else is poor translation."
>
> — Rumi

Afterwards

Feel the subtle shift of consciousness within, the space between "can" and "cannot." Notice how your mind can flow from one possibility to the other or find rest at the neutral point in between.

Allow yourself to inhabit all three positions, tasting how reality can expand when you open to the quantum nature of existence.

Sense yourself as eternally free and abundant. Breathe that truth into your inner reality. Let the certainty of your infinite potential shape your external world.

In this process, recognize that many causes and effects have already been set in motion. Let karma take its natural course while you continue cultivating higher awareness, moving alongside all currents without getting caught in their turbulence.

Remain vigilant against lower vibrations. Use them as opportunities to deepen in meditation and wisdom rather than allowing them to dictate your life. As you rise above limiting thoughts and quiet the mind, you begin to see the intricate play of energies uniting all things.

Pause, take a slow breath, and exhale with grace and gratitude. Even if you can sustain this clear and luminous state for only a few minutes, it will begin to transform your perception.

Remember, the universe is fundamentally magical, and you need only trust and feel its currents. Follow whatever is truly beneficial for you, guided by a broader vision and the call of your heart.

Allow regular meditation to open your intuitive channels. Honor and follow these messages wholeheartedly, trusting that your life is unfolding according to a greater plan and that you are fully supported.

Place your faith in the choices you make, adapting to each new circumstance with gratitude. In doing so, you reinforce your understanding that you are, at your core, boundless consciousness.

Through continuous practice, patience, and trust, the world itself will reveal its interconnectedness, and your life will reflect the expanse of your awakened state.

You are seeking financial independence, but why not aim for financial freedom? Expand your consciousness. There is more for All.

Note to the Reader: The neutral point is emptiness, luminous and beyond description. It is not one, not two. Like a light bulb that is on or off, but beyond both is the shattering of the bulb itself. A sudden pfff, a burst, a release, a dissolving into vast space. No boundaries. No center. Only pure awareness. And from that space, you return more aware.

The greatest illusion is that life is divided into past and future, into spirit and matter, into heaven and earth. But this division exists only in perception, like the difference between open and closed eyes.

With eyes open, we see form, movement, cause and effect. With eyes closed, we feel silence, depth, and the infinite. Yet, nothing changes between the two states except awareness.

The manifest and the unmanifest are not opposites; they are the same reality, shifting like breath, in and out, being and non-being.

Ancient myths whisper this truth to those who listen. Tiamat, the great chaos, was not destroyed. She became creation itself. The world was not made from her defeat but from her transformation.

Likewise, Adam and Eve were never truly cast out of paradise. They merely began to see division where before there was only unity.

The mind splits existence into before and after, creator and destroyer, self and other. But look deeper and you will see. Nothing has ever been separate.

There is no afterlife waiting to be earned. There is no heaven beyond this moment, no hell to escape. Heaven and hell are only states of mind, born from how you see and live.

To seek salvation elsewhere is to deny the life already in your hands. This moment is eternity. The now is the only truth.

What you do here and now is your eternity.

Do not wait for destiny. Do not seek purpose in some distant future. You are the creator, the preserver, the transformer.

The One has already broken into the many, yet the many are still the One. When you see this, fear dissolves. Death loses its grip. Every breath becomes sacred.

The cosmos breathes in and out. Existence and nonexistence. Form and formless. Seen and unseen.

But it is always the same breath. The same life. You are not apart from it. Whether your eyes are open or closed, it remains. Reality simply is. Live it fully. Now.

> "You are alive, so trust life's embrace.
> If heaven exists, bring it to this place."

"I am wiser than this man, for neither of us knows anything great and good; but he fancies he knows something, although he knows nothing, whereas I, as I do not know anything, do not fancy I do."

– Plato, Apology 21d

All that matters is how you treat yourself and others, for there is no separation, just as there is no division between This and That. So the question remains, what kind of world do you want to create?

All is not two.

The Centerless Center

Is there a creator God? Ultimately, it depends on the level from which we ask this question.

On the highest level of nondual understanding, there is no creation at all because there is no separation: no distinction between Purusha and Prakriti, no separation of Shiva and Shakti, no gulf between Father and Mother, no line between the Masculine and Feminine energies.

All dissolves into an emptiness so complete that the very notions of a "creator" and a "creation" lose all meaning.

Yet on the earthly plane, one might answer "yes," there is a God. But how that God is conceived remains elusive, for the Source, the Tao, cannot be fully defined.

Whether God is seen as separate from creation or one with it depends on the lens through which we look, and no single view can fully contain the mystery. Or we can say, God is at once the Architect, the Actor, the Audience — and none of these at all.

Throughout the world's wisdom traditions, people have chosen countless Ishtadevatas, personal deities or divine forms, according to their needs and inclinations.

We are free to embrace a form that resonates with our hearts. What truly matters is that we never impose our personal vision of the Divine upon others, nor should we allow our own understanding to become fixed or dogmatic.

Any time we try to pinpoint and codify the Source, it eventually crystallizes into ego and structure. Both must be broken down again and again. That is why we must realize:

"Do without source. Act from the heart."

The painful process arises because as soon as we make something the Source, it becomes an idea, an ego, a structure.

Yet for the untrained mind, having a temporary point of devotion, an Ishtadevata, is sometimes necessary. It offers stability until one is ready to surrender even that.

Through repeated cycles of formation and dissolution, we begin to glimpse the luminous emptiness at the heart of all things. In the Guhyasamaja Tantra, three profound principles offer guidance:

- **Prajna is Shunyata** – Wisdom is Emptiness

- **Upaya is Karuna** – Method is Compassion

- **Kriya is Vajra** – Power is Activity

These three are not separate. They arise together like light, warmth, and movement from a single flame.

When we see clearly that all things are empty and ever changing, wisdom gives birth to compassion, because there is no rigid self or other to defend.

From this compassion flows the strength to act, not from ego or control, but from the natural stillness of the heart.

Wisdom without compassion becomes cold, compassion without wisdom can become confused, and action without both is blind.

But when wisdom sees emptiness, compassion opens, and action becomes pure and unstoppable like thunder.

In their union, life becomes a sacred dance, clear in mind, open in heart, and fearless in movement.

In this view, emptiness does not mean nothingness. It means all phenomena, including the mind, lack a fixed, independent core.

Whenever we try to define or locate a final source or "origin," we create mental constructions that feed the ego.

Letting go of these constructs is not a retreat into a void but a release from false boundaries. Emptiness remains a mystery beyond conceptual grasp, yet it reveals the interdependence of all things.

Realizing this frees us from clinging, awakens compassion, and allows us to live with clarity and love in every moment.

Looking to Western philosophy, in Ecce Homo, Nietzsche contrasts Dionysus and the Crucified. He seeks to move beyond conventional morality and celebrates the Dionysian spirit.

Yet he does not see that to truly transcend duality and give birth to something higher, the time must come for Dionysus to be crucified as well, held between opposites.

The cross symbolizes this tension of breaking and remaking, the alchemical process of Solve et Coagula, where old forms dissolve so a new reality can emerge as the Übermensch.

Whether viewed through Eastern or Western lenses, every image, concept, or form is only a doorway to something greater.

Let us now look through the lens of Eastern wisdom, turning to Kaivalya Pada, Sutra 33, the final verse of Patanjali's Yoga Sutras as translated by Swami Vivekananda, where the journey ends and the Self stands free.

> The resolution in the inverse order of the qualities, bereft of any motive of action for the Purusa, is Kaivalya, or it is the establishment of the power of knowledge in its own nature.

Nature's task is done, this unselfish task which our sweet nurse, Nature, had imposed upon herself.

As it were, she gently took the self-forgetting soul by the hand, and showed him all the experiences in the universe, all manifestations, bringing him higher and higher through various bodies, till his glory came back, and he remembered his own nature.

Then the kind mother went back the way she came, for others who have also lost their way in the trackless desert of life.

And thus she is working, without beginning and without end. And thus through pleasure and pain, through good and evil, the infinite river of souls is flowing into the ocean of perfection, of self-realisation.

Glory unto those who have realised their own nature! May their blessings be on us all!

- Kaivalya literally means "aloneness" or "absolute independence," but in Yoga philosophy it points to the supreme state of liberation where the *Purusha* stands in its own true nature, not entangled with the mind or body.

- It is the realization that we are not the body or mind, but the unchanging witness behind it all.

- Swami Vivekananda describes it as returning to our original divine nature, in which we become fully aware that we *were always free*, and the movements of Nature were just lessons along the way.

- At this point, the sense of separation and limitation dissolves, and we rest in our own self-luminous consciousness— complete, peaceful, and ever-free.

In the end, love and compassion rooted in presence go beyond all intellectual conclusions. Only through the heart can we sense the living mystery that holds everything together, free of all notions of beginning and end, and fully alive in the n0w.

> "The mind is its own place, and in itself can make a heaven of hell, a hell of heaven.."
>
> — John Milton, Paradise Lost

All attempts to define or locate a final source inevitably dissolve, for the universal is beyond concept.

Emptiness is not a void but the radiant interdependence that reveals itself in every breath, gesture, and moment of stillness.

The mind, ever-seeking to categorize and control, forgets this vast simplicity. Yet within the quiet space of presence, the heart remains open, knowing without the need for proof.

Whatever the mind neglects in its restless pursuit of certainty, the heart continues to hold in silent, unbroken awareness.

The heart knows... what the mind forgets. The heart knows.

The Bindu

I wear no veil, for I am flame.
I dance in silence, beyond all name.
What you fear to show, I set free.
In naked truth, you become Me.
Now rise, as fire, as love, as seed.
I walk with you, where light and shadow meet

The Bindu
Oh The Bindu
Hum Hum Hum

Drop every concept of God
Every shape, every name, every imagined throne.
Let it all dissolve like a wave returning to the sea.

What remains is not a deity, but a dot.
A Bindu: silent, undivided, unborn.
The center of all things and yet no thing at all.

Surrender to that.

Not to a story.
Not to a system.
But to the ungraspable truth pulsing behind your breath.

You are not meant to understand it.
You are meant to **live it**, naked and free.
To meet life not with control, but with presence.

Let your ideas fall like ash.
Let your prayers become silence.
And let that silence become you.

For in that single point
the dot above the arrow,
the stillness after becoming
you will remember:

There is nothing to reach.
Har Har Mukanday.
No goal to attain.

Only Bindu remains
where not two arise,
and all returns to Heart.

Only this:
The great letting go.
The sacred return to the point where all becomes Emptiness.

The Bindu.
Surrender to that.
00:00

Printed in Dunstable, United Kingdom